A TEACHER'S GUIDE TO
USING
LISTED
BUILDINGS

Crispin Keith

English Heritage

CONTENTS

ROYAL COMMISSION ON THE HISTORICAL MONUMENTS OF ENGLAND

**De La Warr
Pavilion, Bexhill-
on-Sea
photographed in
1935. Grade II
listed building.**

ROYAL COMMISSION ON THE HISTORICAL MONUMENTS OF ENGLAND

**Liberty's, Regent
Street, London.
Grade II listed
building.**

ABOUT THIS BOOK

Local listed buildings make an excellent study for schools. They link the present, past and future, and fall within the firsthand experience of pupils. As every locality has listed buildings, this study can be rooted in the pupils' own environment, involving them in the history of their own areas and decisions which affect their own futures. The subject is flexible enough to interest an eight-year-old or stretch an eighteen-year-old. It is genuinely cross-curricular, involving pupils in both practical and theoretical work, getting them out of the classroom and into the community. It is a topic with which pupils may become heavily involved and it can stimulate vehement discussion. It is a direct and tangible route to preparing pupils for citizenship. And, most importantly, it is a fieldwork topic that is cheap and accessible: almost every school will have listed buildings within walking distance.

You may know about the existence of listed buildings but you may not yet have thought about their enormous educational potential. You will find that there is a huge reservoir of goodwill and support, both locally and nationally and from individuals and organisations alike, for any school or pupil that gets involved with conservation issues and listed buildings.

Using listed buildings is exciting. You and your pupils will probably learn together, whilst outsiders such as planners, architects, librarians, archivists, curators, conservationists and ordinary local people become providers. The wide complex issues of the outside world (for example, political, economic and moral dilemmas, conservation, development, pollution) cross curriculum boundaries and will develop questioning attitudes in pupils. All types of media and communication will be involved.

Since the issues and stories are current ones the teacher cannot predict the outcomes, but, most excitingly, pupils who get involved in local planning issues can sometimes influence the outcome themselves.

The purpose of this book is to stimulate and give guidance on the educational use of listed buildings. It aims to inform about the listing process and the issues involved, to suggest ways to research and make use of local buildings, and to give ideas on how to involve pupils of all levels in all areas of the curriculum. Of course, not every idea will be appropriate to your pupils and your local buildings, but with nearly 440,000 listed buildings in England with all the varieties, oddities, intricacies and possibilities that they present, you should be able to find some ways of using your own local buildings.

Some structures are listed for their historical importance or for their unique nature. The Sir Bernard Lovell radio telescope at Jodrell Bank, built in 1952-7, qualifies on both counts. Grade I listed building.

ENGLISH HERITAGE

ABOUT LISTED BUILDINGS

THE HISTORICAL BACKGROUND

Pressure first began to mount for legislation to protect old structures in the late nineteenth century. There are two strands to the legislation that followed over the next hundred years. One strand applies to ancient monuments and the other to historic buildings. This book is concerned with listed buildings, but to set the preservation of historic buildings in context it is necessary to look briefly at the history of the protection of ancient monuments as well.

General Augustus Henry Pitt Rivers (1827-1900), first Inspector of Ancient Monuments.

Government action was, at first, very slow and reluctant; General Pitt Rivers, the first government-appointed Inspector of Ancient Monuments, wrote, 'Government will attend to nothing out of which political capital can not be made, and neither government nor Parliament care a button for ancient monuments.'

Scheduled monuments

Tattershall Castle, Lincolnshire, is a scheduled ancient monument. It was the threat of its removal to the United States that led to the Ancient Monuments Act of 1913.

Alfriston Clergy House is a Grade II* listed building. Photographed here in 1893, it was the first property acquired by the National Trust.

Listed buildings

Historic buildings thought worthy of protection on grounds of special architectural or historic interest are catalogued on a list and known as listed buildings. Because the definition is broader than for scheduled monuments there are far more listed buildings, currently about 440,000.

Listed buildings are more likely than scheduled monuments to be in current use and the majority are private houses. The term actually applies to anything that has been constructed, so lampposts (including those outside No. 10 Downing Street), garden walls, sundials, bridges, bandstands, canal locks and even some tombstones are included.

Ancient monuments of national importance (by reason of their historic, architectural, traditional or archaeological interest) are catalogued on a schedule and are referred to as scheduled monuments. There are about 13,000 scheduled monuments, a tiny proportion of known and unknown archaeological sites.

Scheduled monuments are sites and structures of archaeological importance. Their buried deposits may be as important, if not more so, than any standing remains. Where there are standing remains these are likely to be ruins with no present-day economic use.

The Ancient Monuments Acts of 1882 and 1913 were limited in scope (for instance, all occupied and ecclesiastical buildings were excluded) and provided few means of enforcing protection. The fact that the British government lagged behind most European countries in this area of legislation was due in part to a strong feeling that owners should be at liberty to control their own property, and also to the fear that government commitment to the protection of an unlisted, unquantified built heritage would result in open-ended expenditure.

It was not until 50 years on from the first Ancient Monuments Act that any legal protection was given to historic buildings. 1932 saw the introduction of Building Preservation Orders which local authorities could impose on threatened historic buildings. Only twenty such orders were served, however, before new legislation in 1944. The problem was that local authorities were liable to pay compensation if an owner successfully appealed against an order.

The widespread destruction of buildings by bombing in the Second World War prompted action. In 1941 the National Buildings Record was

set up to compile records of war-damaged buildings and it has continued to this day to record the built heritage. Also in 1941, the Ministry of Works appointed regional panels of architects to draw up the first lists of buildings of architectural and historical importance. This survey took eighteen months.

By 1944 plans were being made for the post-war rebuilding of British cities. The 1944 Town and Country Planning Act brought responsibility for historic buildings under the new Town and Country Planning Ministry, which could compile new lists of historic buildings that local authorities should note when

120,000 historic buildings had been listed, but many thousands of historic buildings had been sacrificed in the reshaping of post-war Britain.

It was perhaps the public perception of the extent of destruction of the built heritage in the 1960s which prompted new legislation that at last really did protect buildings. The Civic Trust had been formed in 1957, the Victorian Society in 1958, and by 1967 there was a flourishing local amenity movement campaigning on local environmental issues. An Act of 1967 introduced Conservation Areas, which gave local authorities the power to designate zones within which they would have statutory

Demolition for development in 1956.

Damage caused by bombing during World War II and the over-zealous efforts of those demolishing unsafe buildings prompted efforts to record and conserve the built heritage. This was a police station in Coventry after a raid in 1941.

preparing their plans. The Act obliged owners of listed buildings to give two months' notice of proposed works. However, it was not until after the 1944 Act was amended in 1947 to make listing a compulsory duty that the listing process began in earnest.

The 1947 Act did not afford much protection to threatened buildings. The lists were only meant as a guide to the local planners and were neither precise nor specific. After 20 years,

powers to control demolition of buildings and walls and the felling of trees. Today there are over 6,000 Conservation Areas in England and 47% of listed buildings are within them.

The 1968 Town and Country Planning Act completely changed the way in which historic buildings were protected. Previously the local authority had had to intervene and risk paying compensation when imposing a Building Preservation Order, but now responsibility lay with the owner of the listed building who had to obtain explicit written consent, called Listed Building Consent, from the local planning authority for any works that would alter the character of the building. The presumption was now that all buildings on the list would be protected. A new listing survey, with far wider criteria, was begun in 1970 in order to make the lists more comprehensive, accurate and precise.

The process was slow and it was only the wrecking of the Firestone Factory over the August Bank Holiday of 1980, and the consequent outrage of the then Secretary of State for the Environment Michael Heseltine, that prompted the Accelerated Resurvey, the most intensive and wide-ranging listing survey to date, employing a field staff of 90. They completed their work in 1987. Buildings continue to be listed with, for example, 6,000 buildings being added to the list in 1989/90.

English Heritage was formed in 1983, and now advises ministers on the listing process in England. Its stated role is 'to bring about the long term conservation and widespread understanding and enjoyment of the historic environment for the benefit of present and future generations using expert advice, education, example, persuasion, intervention and financial support.'

Today, green issues are prominent in the media and in politics, and there is an active conservation movement: the National Trust has 2,000,000 members, English Heritage 250,000 members, and there are many specialist building conservation societies as well as nearly 1,000 local amenity societies with interests in building conservation. All these groups are active in trying to ensure that the community at large actually does protect our built heritage. The outlook today is good: we now have an evolving structure of legislation and lists of buildings, backed by a heightened public awareness, which promises to minimise (but not stop) the loss of what William Morris called 'sacred monuments to the nation's hope and growth'.

Significant dates in the protection of old structures

1882 First Ancient Monuments Protection Act
- established a schedule of monuments that the state should protect
- an Inspector was appointed
- nearly all items on the schedule (29 in England, 21 in Scotland and 18 in Ireland) were prehistoric
- there were no compulsory powers

1894 Survey of London established
- to create a systematic inventory of buildings and monuments in London

1900 Ancient Monuments Amendment Act
- allowed inclusion of Romano-British and medieval monuments on schedule

1908 Royal Commissions set up
- one each for Scotland, England and Wales
- to prepare inventories of structures and sites earlier than 1700 worthy of preservation

1913 Ancient Monuments Consolidation Act
- owners of scheduled monuments to give one month's notice of their intention to carry out work
- Minister could impose a Preservation Order to prevent works
- provided for an Inspectorate
- set up an Advisory Board of academics and experts to advise on criteria for deciding whether a monument was of national importance. They aimed to include in the schedule 'examples from the different periods from the Stone Age to the development of industry'
- occupied houses and ecclesiastical buildings exempted from this legislation

1932 Town and Country Planning Act
- Building Preservation Orders introduced
- to be served by local authorities on threatened historic buildings
- occupied dwelling houses covered for the first time
- compensation to be paid if Minister of Works failed to uphold the Order

1941 National Buildings Record founded

1944 Town and Country Planning Act
- responsibility for historic buildings moved from Ministry of Works to the new Ministry of Town and Country Planning
- lists of historic buildings might be compiled which local authorities should note when preparing plans
- owners of listed buildings to give two months' notice of proposed works

1947 Town and Country Planning Act
- for first time Minister obliged to prepare lists whereas previously this had been optional
- these lists were only advisory and published for the guidance of local authorities
- to protect a building the local authority had to issue a Building Preservation Order

1953 Historic Buildings and Ancient Monuments Act
- introduction of central government grants for the preservation of historic buildings
- Historic Buildings Councils for England, Wales and Scotland established to advise Minister on grants and on listing policy

1962 Local authorities able to offer grants towards the repair of listed buildings

1967 Civic Amenities Act
- Conservation Areas introduced
- underlined the importance of lesser buildings when they were part of a group

1968 Town and Country Planning Act
- for first time all buildings on the list given statutory protection
- owner now had to obtain Listed Building Consent from the local planning authority for works which would alter the building's character

1970 Resurvey begins
- need for far greater precision

1971 Town and Country Planning Act
- allowed local authorities to designate conservation areas
- local authorities permitted to serve repairs notices on owners of listed buildings and to follow up with compulsory purchase where necessary

1974 Specific consent required to demolish buildings in conservation areas

1980 Firestone Factory wrecked over a bank holiday

1980 Rapid listing of 150 1920s and 1930s buildings

1982 Accelerated resurvey begins

1983 National Heritage Act
- English Heritage established
- Secretary of State for the Environment obliged to consult English Heritage on listing matters, and to refer certain applications for listed building consent for advice
- Historic Buildings Council for England wound up

1987 Resurvey completed

1989 Review of early resurvey lists begins
- emphasis on close co-operation with local communities
- listing workshop meetings held

1990 Planning (Listed Buildings and Conservation Areas) Act 1990
- brings together and tidies up all previous legislation so that general planning legislation separated from conservation legislation

WHAT ARE LISTED BUILDINGS?

There are about 440,000 listed buildings in England which appear on a register recording buildings of special architectural or historical interest. This list is split into three categories.

Grade I - about 6,000 buildings (or 2% of listed buildings) defined as being of 'exceptional interest'. These include the outstanding churches and cathedrals, great country houses like Audley End and Blenheim, town planning set pieces like the Royal Crescent, Bath, and a variety of public buildings, such as Leeds Town Hall and Blackpool Tower.

Royal Crescent, Bath. Grade I listed buildings.

Interior of No.6 Royal Crescent, Bath, in 1945. Listing protects the inside as well as the exterior of a building. Grade I listed building.

Grade II* - about 20,000 buildings (or 4% of listed buildings) defined as being of 'more than special interest'.

No.12 Park Village West, Regents Park, London. Grade II* listed building.

Grade II - over 94% of listed buildings defined as being of 'special interest'.

The Department of the Environment gives a broad definition of what, on the advice of English Heritage, it lists:

■ all buildings built before 1700 which survive in anything like their original condition

■ most buildings of 1700 to 1840, though selection is necessary

■ between 1840 and 1914 only buildings of definite quality and character, and the selection is designed to include the principal

works of the principal architects

■ between 1914 and 1939 selected buildings of high quality or historic interest

■ a few outstanding buildings erected after 1939

In choosing buildings, particular attention is paid to:

■ special value within certain types, either for architectural or planning reasons or as illustrating social and economic history (for instance, industrial buildings, railway stations, schools, hospitals, theatres, town halls, markets, exchanges, almshouses, prisons, lock-ups, mills)

■ technological innovation or virtuosity (for instance cast iron, prefabrication, or the early use of concrete)

■ association with well-known characters or events

■ group value, especially as examples of town planning (for instance, squares, terraces or model villages)

Cromwell Place, St Ives, Cambridgeshire. Grade II listed buildings.

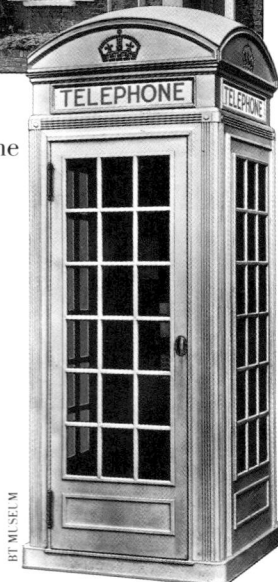

Some old types of telephone box are rare, and are listed.

Malt Mill Lane, Alcester, Warwickshire, photographed in 1964. These modest buildings have been listed for their group value: their scale, use of materials and age are important to the street as a whole. The alteration of any one of these houses would destroy the harmony of the row.

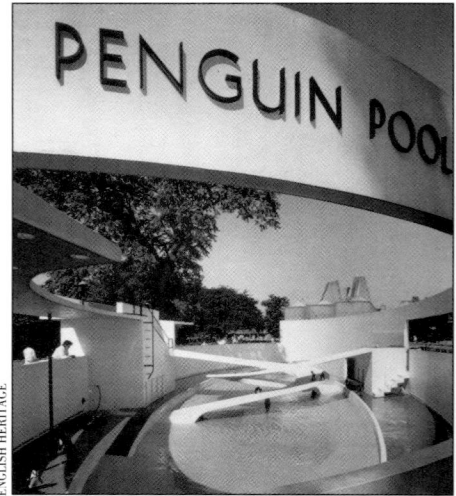

The Penguin Pool at London Zoo, designed by Lubetkin in 1933-4, uses reinforced concrete. Grade I listed building.

The Palm House, Kew Gardens, is an example of the use of cast iron and glass. Grade I listed building.

THE LISTING PROCESS

Most listed buildings have been selected in the national surveys, the latest of which was completed in 1987. However, if it is considered that a building has been overlooked by the surveys, it can be 'spot listed'. If a building is threatened the local authority can protect it quickly by serving a building preservation notice. This gives the building temporary listed status for up to six months, in which time a decision on listing must be made. Spot listing is usually initiated by a local authority or a local amenity society but, in fact, anyone can apply to the Department of the Environment for a

However, if their application fails the buildings may be added to the statutory list.

Once a building is listed the local authority must inform the owners and occupiers of the building. The Department of the Environment will consider requests for buildings to be de-listed if new evidence can be produced to show that the building does not possess the special architectural or historic interest ascribed to it.

Listed buildings are included in a Department of the Environment 'greenback'. These green-covered books are the lists which give a short description of each listed building in a borough or district. The listed

I: Interior
S: Subsidiary features, such as railings or outbuildings
H: History of the building relevant to listing
E: Extra information relevant to listing
S: Sources of information

Not all these headings will be used for all buildings listed.

An entry from a list showing what each section of the entry means.

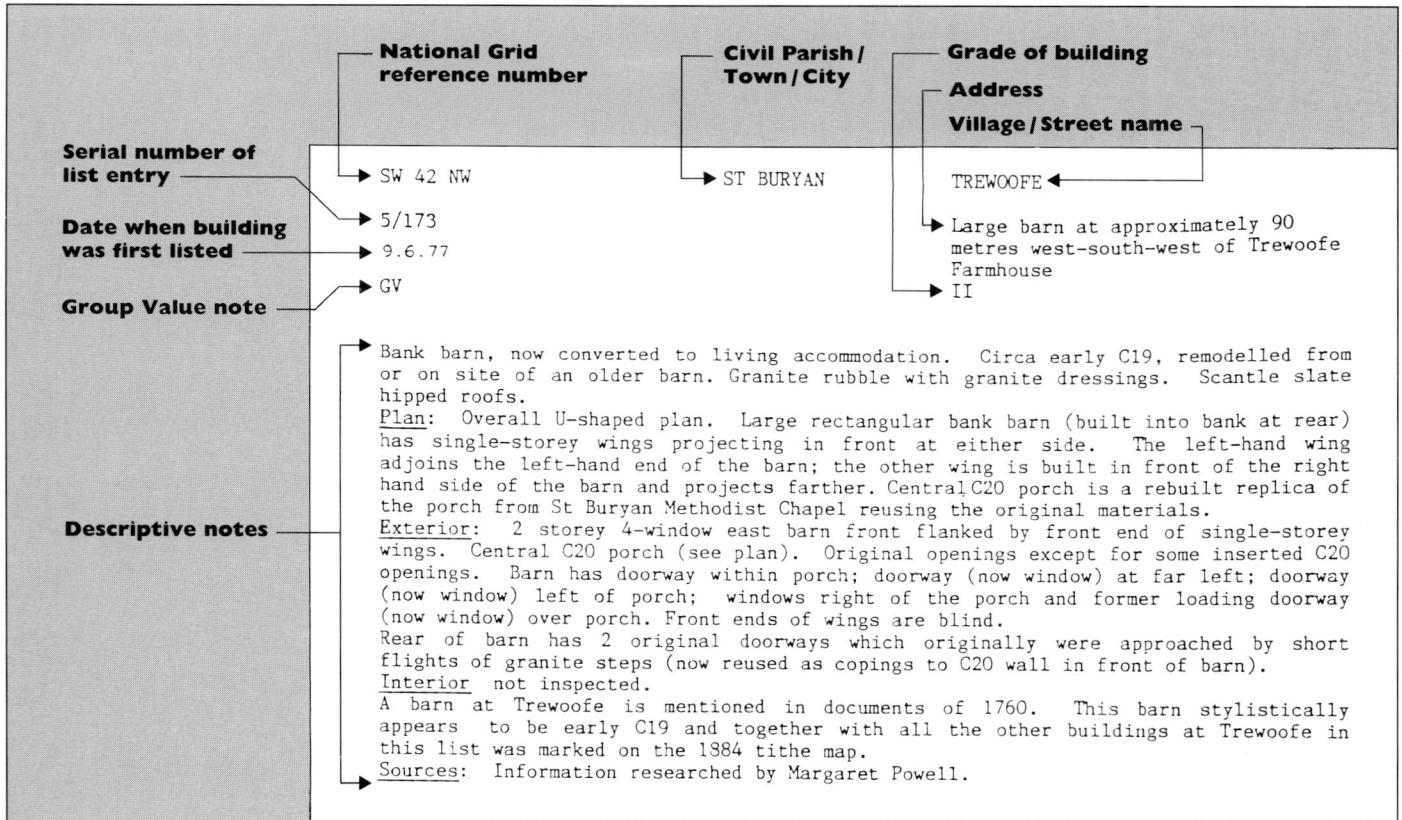

Serial number of list entry	National Grid reference number	Civil Parish / Town / City	Grade of building
			Address
			Village / Street name

SW 42 NW → ST BURYAN → TREWOOFE ←

Date when building was first listed → 5/173

9.6.77 → Large barn at approximately 90 metres west-south-west of Trewoofe Farmhouse

Group Value note → GV → II

Descriptive notes →

Bank barn, now converted to living accommodation. Circa early C19, remodelled from or on site of an older barn. Granite rubble with granite dressings. Scantle slate hipped roofs.
Plan: Overall U-shaped plan. Large rectangular bank barn (built into bank at rear) has single-storey wings projecting in front at either side. The left-hand wing adjoins the left-hand end of the barn; the other wing is built in front of the right hand side of the barn and projects farther. Central C20 porch is a rebuilt replica of the porch from St Buryan Methodist Chapel reusing the original materials.
Exterior: 2 storey 4-window east barn front flanked by front end of single-storey wings. Central C20 porch (see plan). Original openings except for some inserted C20 openings. Barn has doorway within porch; doorway (now window) at far left; doorway (now window) left of porch; windows right of the porch and former loading doorway (now window) over porch. Front ends of wings are blind.
Rear of barn has 2 original doorways which originally were approached by short flights of granite steps (now reused as copings to C20 wall in front of barn).
Interior not inspected.
A barn at Trewoofe is mentioned in documents of 1760. This barn stylistically appears to be early C19 and together with all the other buildings at Trewoofe in this list was marked on the 1884 tithe map.
Sources: Information researched by Margaret Powell.

---

building to be listed as long as they send a full set of photographs, maps and explanations as to why the building should be listed.

Developers, worried that buildings they are working on might get listed midway through their project so halting their work, may apply for a Certificate of Immunity from listing, stating that it is not intended to list the buildings shown in the application plans for five years. This gives developers the certainty they need before proceeding with work.

buildings are arranged by address.

The most recent listings give more information than previously, organised under headings with the mnemonic B DAMP FISHES. This stands for:

B: Building type: original purpose and present function
D: Date, or dates, of different parts
A: Architect / Craftsman / Patron
M: Materials
P: Plan and style
F: Facade

LISTED BUILDING CONTROL

The register of listed buildings exists in order to identify our cultural, social and architectural historical heritage. However, the list does more than just identify special buildings: it is used to protect them.

The demolition, alteration to the interior or exterior, or extension of a listed building can be authorised only by a specific grant of Listed Building Consent by the local authority. Listed

Building Consent is also required for any alterations that would change the character of a listed building: this may include replacement of traditional-style windows with those of a modern style or painting walls an unusual colour. Local planning authorities must advertise any such applications that they receive and must display a notice on or near the relevant site. The public may then make representations of which the authority must take account before making any decision to grant Listed Building Consent. Once the authority has decided to grant Listed Building Consent they must, in some cases, notify the Secretary of State, who can decide whether or not he should call in the application for his own decision. In all considerations the presumption is in favour of preservation unless a strong case can be made for change.

An owner who demolishes a listed building without Listed Building Consent faces an unlimited fine and up to a year's imprisonment, though such penalties are seldom imposed. Owners of listed buildings also have a duty to look after them; they can apply for repair grants from English Heritage or the local authority, but if they allow a listed building to fall into disrepair, the local authority can issue the owner with an urgent repairs notice specifying what repairs must be carried out. If this work is not done, the local authority, with permission from the Department of the Environment, may buy the building with a compulsory purchase order. The local authority is then responsible for the upkeep of the building. In the rare cases where local authorities have failed themselves to look after listed or compulsorily purchased buildings, the Secretary of State has exercised his powers to compel local authorities to carry out their duties.

In all but the most extreme cases such safeguards are not used. Few applications for Listed Building Consent are refused outright; usually the legislation is used to control development through a process of negotiation and modification. Hence consent for alterations may be granted subject to conditions set by the local authority.

Is this protection effective? In 1988, 185 listed buildings were permitted to be demolished, most having been judged to be 'beyond reasonable economic use', but, on the other hand, no Grade I listed building has been lost in the last ten years.

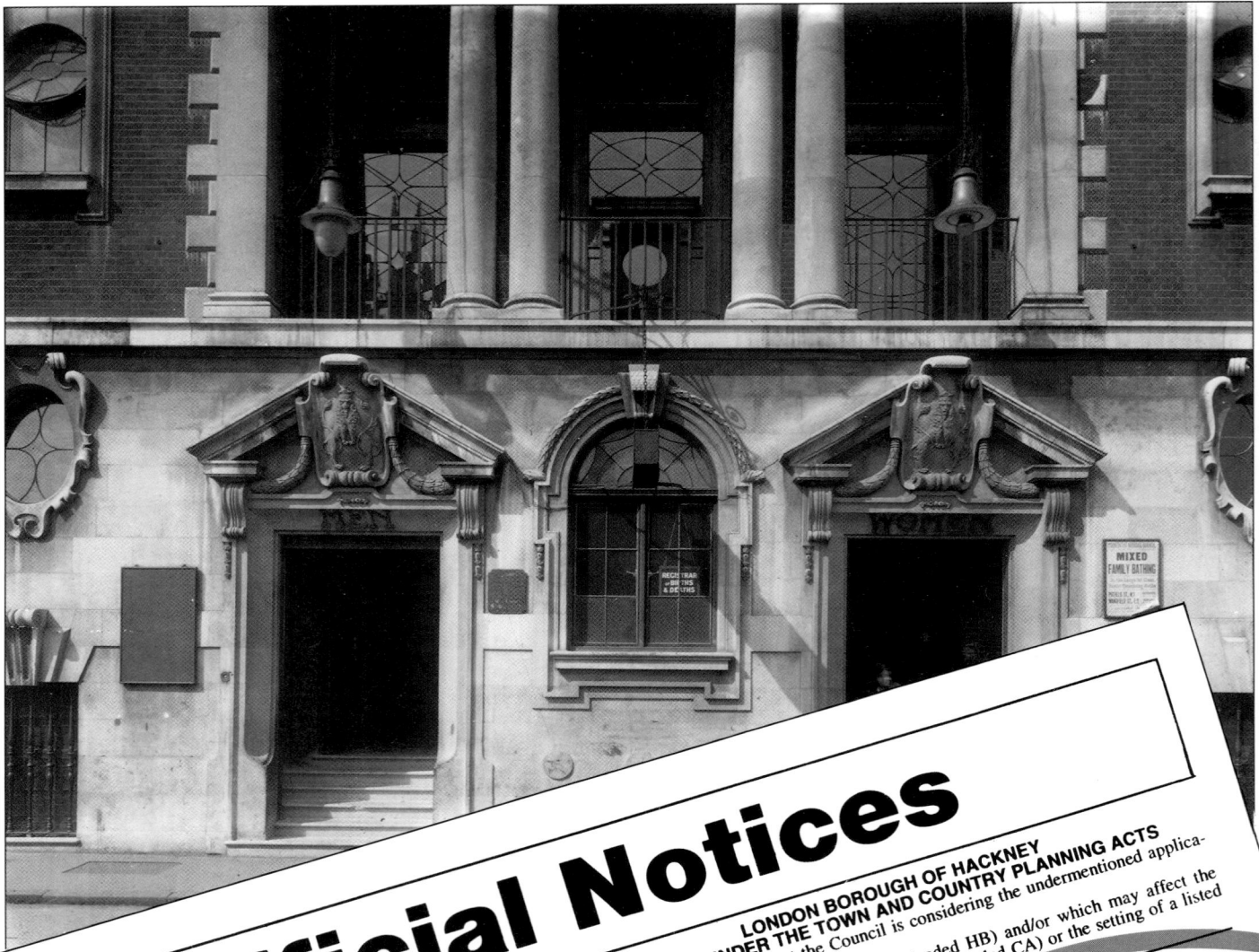

Official Notices

LONDON BOROUGH OF HACKNEY
NOTICE UNDER THE TOWN AND COUNTRY PLANNING ACTS

Notice is hereby given that the Council is considering the undermentioned applica-

Description of Development

Town and Country Planning Act 1990
Country Planning General Regu-

LONDON BOROUGH OF HACKNEY
NOTICE UNDER THE TOWN AND COUNTRY PLANNING ACTS

Notice is hereby given that the Council is considering the undermentioned applications:-

Applications for listed building consent (coded HB) and/or which may affect the character or appearance of a conservation area (coded CA) or the setting of a listed building (coded setting HB)

Code	Address	Description of Development
HB	Haggerston Pool Whiston Road, E2 21-25 Earl Street, EC2	Removal of 12 slipper baths together with the installation of a Sauna and Showers. Use of basement and ground floor as restaurant/take-away and alteration to front elevation at ground level. Continued use as a Turkish Sports Club. Continued use as a Turkish Sports Club.
CA	Place, E5	

These sorts of statistics suggest that the legislation is very effective but they do not reflect the real threat to our historic buildings. Today this comes not from demolition but from two other sources: slow decay and inappropriate alteration. It is estimated that about 9% of listed buildings are currently out of use and therefore particularly vulnerable to gradual deterioration. They are classified by English Heritage as 'Buildings at Risk' and, like for example maltings or workhouses, are often no longer needed for their original purpose. Local planning authorities are being encouraged to make registers of buildings at risk and to concentrate their efforts on developing creative schemes, often in partnership with developers, to attempt to reverse the decline.

ROYAL COMMISSION ON THE HISTORICAL MONUMENTS OF ENGLAND

This Grade II listed building in Brighton with its rounded bay and mathematical tiles (made to look like brick) is in serious danger from neglect.

ARCHITECTURAL ASSOCIATION AND ANDREW HIGGOTT

Inappropriate alteration.

The other threat is almost more insidious and comes from the gradual accumulation of inappropriate alterations such as insensitive window and door replacements and inappropriate pointing or surface detail. Such small-scale but widespread change is difficult to monitor and control and yet can completely change the character of buildings.

Listed Building Consent in Greater London

There is one way in which listed building control is treated differently in London. The 33 London Boroughs act as local planning authorities but the Greater London Council, as the strategic planning authority, was given powers to direct London Boroughs to refuse applications for Listed Building Consent. When the GLC ceased to exist in 1986 these powers passed to English Heritage.

Churches, chapels and cathedrals

Churches, chapels and cathedrals are listed in the same way as any other building. All ecclesiastical buildings are exempt from listed building control. Because the Church of England is the established church, however, the Anglican Church has its own systems to deal with listed buildings.

THE ISSUES

This chapter outlines some of the issues related to listed buildings which could provide the basis for pupils' discussions and involvement. It aims to draw attention to these issues rather than to answer all the questions raised by them.

WHAT IS CONSERVATION?

The conservation of buildings raises complex issues. The options may include preserving a building in the state in which it was found, recycling or adapting a building for new uses, restoring a building to its original state using traditional or modern techniques, or substantial rebuilding. Conservation can even encompass the detailed recording of a building before it is demolished, or the placing of a plaque on the site of a demolished building. All of these processes can be appropriate in certain circumstances, but argument arises over specific cases and over where the emphasis of long-term policies should lie.

Should the emphasis of conservation policy, for example, be on preserving buildings as they are found, or on conserving them by recycling and adapting for a new use? Critics of preservation say it leads to sterile museum-like attractions that are dead when people aren't visiting them. Robert Hewison, in *The Heritage Industry*, argues that an obsession with the past will prevent Britain from developing into the modern world, and suggests that an emphasis on preservation often sanitizes and thus distorts our view of the past: we don't preserve the filthy and uncomfortable conditions of the past, but often retain just the acceptable and the romantic. On the other hand tourism is a dynamic force for development, and lively popular presentations of our heritage do interest and educate a large and vital section of the population. It is also clear that there are some buildings which cannot easily be reused sympathetically or

ENGLISH HERITAGE

St Mark's, North Audley Street, London: hamburger restaurant or gallery?

ENGLISH HERITAGE

Truman's Brewery, Brick Lane, London. Grade II listed building.

economically, in which case a deep-freeze solution may be preferable to demolition.

Conservation by adaptation to meet current needs can also be controversial. It is always a subjective choice as to whether the new function of a building is appropriate, and adaptation, because it involves change, will often provoke opposition. St Mark's Church, North Audley Street, was destined to become a hamburger restaurant until public opposition put a stop to the plans. Proposed change of use to an art gallery was not resisted so vociferously. Quite substantial changes have been necessary to turn the

Truman Brewery in Spitalfields into offices. It is an eye-catching building that makes its own contribution to the local environment but there is no doubt that the character of the building has been radically altered in the process.

Restoration becomes controversial when new techniques or materials are used, or when the plans rely on conjectural reconstructions. With the restoration of the part of Hampton Court destroyed by fire, the debate was between the use of steel (for convenience) or timber (for authenticity) for the construction of roof trusses; timber was eventually used. Uppark House, extensively damaged by fire in 1989, is to be restored by the National Trust and re-opened to the public. Although the house will no longer be an authentic eighteenth-century house, enough was recovered for an authoritative reconstruction of the ground floor but not of the upper floors. Opinions have varied as to whether a reconstruction of the original stairs should be attempted.

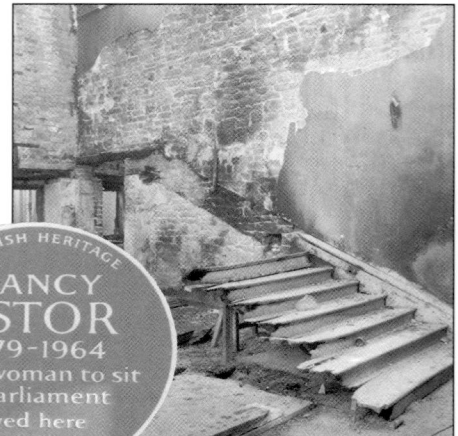

ENGLISH HERITAGE

NANCY ASTOR 1879-1964 First woman to sit in Parliament lived here

Plaque to Nancy Astor at No.4, St James Square, London. Blue plaques commemorate and therefore, in a way, conserve the historical heritage of buildings.

The interior of Uppark House, West Sussex, October 1990, after the devastation of a fire the previous year. Should the burnt staircase be replaced by a facsimile, or by a new design?

Conservation at any price?

No.3 High Street, Hereford could be considered the ultimate example of insensitive conservation: a timber-frame facade raised a storey and shoved over a Littlewoods shop-front with no provision for access, conserving it but making it look ridiculous.

No.3 High Street, Hereford, photographed in 1953 in its original position, next to the chemists. Grade II listed building.

No.3 High Street, Hereford, in final position.

Even conservation by the placing of plaques can cause controversy. The placement of official blue historic plaques in London is controlled by English Heritage, but recently there has been a proliferation of other plaques about the country; some may contend that 'Catherine Cookson country' plaques could trivialise the process, whilst others may argue that they add to the public enjoyment of the built environment.

SHOULD CONSERVATION BE ENFORCED?

There is a body of argument that suggests that conservation and development are natural processes best left to market forces, and that conservation legislation is a bureaucratic strait-jacket reflecting the views and tastes of a minority and giving an artificial unrepresentative view of a Britain frozen in time. Holders of such views argue that

Satellite dishes are attacked by many as being eyesores. Should people be restricted in their TV viewing by the type of house in which they live?

buildings that we value enough will be kept, and that buildings that were well constructed will last, while changes will properly and naturally occur when buildings outlast their use. They point out that no building, however well conserved, will last for ever, and ask why we should try to prolong buildings' lives artificially. Critics of legislation often judge that the twentieth century, with all its planning restrictions, is leaving a far poorer architectural legacy than previous unrestricted eras of development.

These views may well strike a chord with many pupils but such opinions tend to focus on the present situation, without thinking about the future. Without bureaucratic controls, decisions would be based on potential profits, usually short-term profits, made by investors who may not live in the locality or have an interest in the long-term future welfare of the area. Thus planning controls can be seen as guarding the future welfare of a locality, as well as representing the environmental considerations involved in development. Developers and architects die, and their companies go bankrupt, but their artefacts may survive centuries.

Arguments against enforced conservation often neglect the fact that much demolition does not occur for good economic reasons but because of a lack of imagination or a lack of information about the benefits of reusing old buildings. Listing is not a bar to development; it is a process ensuring negotiation and consultation that can result in a compromise benefitting all parties. The twentieth century, with its expanding population and rapidly changing technology and lifestyles, has produced unprecedented strains on our built environment, and legislation is just one way of coping with some of them.

Listed buildings constitute less than 2% of the total building stock. It is hard to argue that restrictions on such a small proportion of buildings represent a significant imposition on society. Such buildings can be viewed as a finite, fragile cultural resource, important to the society that protects them.

CRITERIA FOR CONSERVATION

The criteria for listing clearly set out that buildings to be conserved by law should be of special architectural or historic interest. All pre-1700 intact buildings come into this classification, but for all buildings after 1700 someone has to make a judgement on their listing, and although there are objective criteria to use, different people will define 'special architectural or historic interest' in different ways. There are also criteria for accepting or rejecting proposals to demolish or change buildings already listed, but personal judgement is still needed to apply the criteria. Sir Hugh Casson has asked '... is it true that buildings are often being preserved today not so much for their architectural merit as through fear of what should replace them? And if this indeed be so, is it due to greater visual sensitivity or to lack of confidence, to a more sophisticated awareness or just nostalgia masquerading as architectural compassion?' (from *The future of the past*). So - is conservation purely negative?

Casson, together with Sir Nikolaus Pevsner and Sir John Betjeman and others, held the view, influential in the 1960s, that aesthetic values are more important than the historical values of buildings, that the look of the environment is more important than preserving buildings as social documents or tourist attractions. Critics of this view stress that aesthetic values vary from person to person and decade to decade: it would be too late for the twenty-first century to rediscover a liking for a particular earlier style if that style had been thought so ugly that all examples of it had been demolished in the intervening years.

Today, a vigorous debate is on between the 'modernists' such as developer Peter Palumbo, who press for dynamic innovations in architecture to enhance the environment, and 'classicists' such as Prince Charles, who argue for the retention of accepted traditional or popular building forms. Modernists and classicists would disagree on the aesthetic merits of many buildings proposed for conservation. However,

DOUBLEDAY

Prince Charles argues for traditional approaches to building.

such disagreements are not clear cut: there are no universally accepted definitions of what building styles are 'popular', 'traditional' or 'innovative'.

Does old equal good? Ask most younger pupils which local houses they like and they will often pick out modern houses. Their reasons will centre on cleanliness, size and even status. Children value newness and often reject second-hand possessions. Ask the same question of teachers and the answer is likely to be very different, with the older buildings often being valued for aesthetic or traditional reasons. Is either view 'right'? Should we teach children to value old buildings, or to evaluate them?

HULTON PICTURE COMPANY

Euston Arch, photographed in 1954, demolished 1962.

Is our reverence for old buildings merely a passing phase? Prime Minister Harold Macmillan insisted on the destruction of the Euston Arch in 1962 because he felt 'concern for such relics would sap national vitality'. Later, Prime Minister Harold Wilson claimed, 'All over the country the grime, muddle and decay of our

Victorian heritage is being replaced, and the quality of urban life uplifted.' Should we value buildings not even valued greatly by their original builders, such as those labourers' dwellings built hurriedly and cheaply at the start of the industrial revolution?

If we do value buildings because they're old, does it mean that the older they are, the more important they are? In Chester, proposals to demolish the Georgian listed building

NEWCASTLE CITY LIBRARIES AND ARTS

What makes a building historically important? These Newcastle slums, photographed in the 1870s, were probably not intended by their builders to be monuments to their age, so should they be conserved as such? Some people feel that such buildings are a shameful reminder of a bad past and should be demolished. Others say they should be conserved for precisely the same reason.

Dee House, in order to develop the site of the Roman amphitheatre, were agreed by the Secretary of State after a public inquiry. It has been proposed that the listed buildings of the Georgian Anchor Terrace in London be demolished to allow excavation of the remnants of Shakespeare's Globe Theatre.

Today's perceived vandalism may be the future heritage; today we value highly the same shop-fronts that Dickens, in *Sketches by Boz*, wrote about so scathingly 150 years ago:

From time to time an epidemic breaks out in various trades causing the victims to run stark, raving mad. The symptoms are a love of plate glass, gilding and gas lights. A few years previously there was a nasty outbreak among drapers and haberdashers, but after a while the disease had died away. There was a year or two of quiet and then suddenly it burst out again among chemists, and the symptoms were the same; bright new shop fronts, and then the hosiers were infected and began to pull their shop fronts down with frantic recklessness. The mania began to die away and the public began to congratulate themselves on its entire disappearance when the disease burst forth again with tenfold violence among publicans.

The debate about replacement windows continues today; some owners of listed buildings complain that they are not allowed to replace their old wooden sash windows with uPVC, while conservationists are dismayed by inappropriate modern windows in old buildings and point out that traditional wooden windows, properly maintained, are more practical and economical than uPVC.

Should people be allowed to alter terrace houses to suit their own taste?

There can also be problems agreeing on what makes a building historically important, in the same way that there is controversy on what history is important enough to be taught in schools. Political beliefs may influence whether buildings documenting the past exploitation of the working class, or demonstrating the artistic benefits of patronage by the rich, are the more important to keep. Former Portsmouth MP Mike Hancock urged the demolition of a listed former workhouse with the words, 'I think the building is a throw-back to a best-forgotten era ...'

The Department of the Environment Circular 8/87 emphasizes that 'historic buildings ... are vitally important to the environmental quality of life in this country.' But what happens when local people believe that their environment would be improved by the removal of a historic building? Power stations, a cast-iron urinal and blockhouses have all been listed for their historical importance and yet they may not be the types of building that obviously enhance the environment. Imaginative, sensitive adaptation is the conservationists' solution to this dilemma, but it is hard to see how Calder Hall, historically important as an early nuclear power station, can be sensitively adapted to enhance the environment.

The conservation of buildings should also take into account irrational criteria such as people's emotional attachment to familiar settings; the destruction of familiar or loved buildings can be deeply upsetting, especially for old people, but it is hard to quantify or anticipate such effects, and even harder to set emotional criteria against those of architecture and history.

Differing opinions as to what constitutes architectural merit or historical importance are likely to be underpinned by differing opinions on the ultimate aims of building conservation. Conservation is undertaken because it helps to define our national, local or individual identities, because it makes good economic or environmental sense, and because it may help us to learn lessons for the future. Few people would argue with any of these

justifications, but agreement on the relative importance of each is harder to achieve.

CONFLICTING INTERESTS

In a Commons debate on property development around St Paul's in the City of London, in May 1989, Labour MP Tony Banks said, 'I don't see why a bunch of property speculators, behaving like up-market Arthur Daleys, should be allowed to put their profits before our history.' Virginia Bottomley, Under Secretary of State, replied, 'There is always a tension as

St Paul's Cathedral in 1974, obscured by modern development. The built environment is also threatened by the increasing volume of traffic.

to how much we should preserve: do we want London to be a modern living city, or a square mile of archaeological remains?' A few months later a TV programme ran a spoof story that St Paul's was to be demolished because it didn't fit in with the buildings around it! This example may give an over-polarized picture of heritage and developers in conflict, but the City of London is an area where many conflicting interests compete. The solution to the problem must take into consideration far more than just the historical and architectural heritage: worsening traffic congestion, concerns about pollution, increased demand for office space, increased tourism and important financial considerations are all of relevance.

Conflicting interests are not confined to wealthy areas like the City of London: changes may be vital to the economic regeneration of run-down areas, but such development may demand new supermarkets, factories or leisure complexes where listed buildings now stand. The motor vehicle, unknown when most listed buildings were constructed, now requires widened streets, bypasses, parking spaces, and the strengthening of old buildings vulnerable to the vibrations of traffic. Calne, Wiltshire, lost many buildings with the widening of the A4, destruction that proved unnecessary once the M4 had been built. The need for car parks has also clashed with conservation in towns such as Beverley and Cheltenham.

Many pupils will side with the everyday requirements of local inhabitants: to them the obvious advantages of absence of traffic jams, easy parking, shopping malls, and a new swimming pool or cinema may far outweigh abstract, aesthetic or historical reasons for conserving an old building. Promoting the economic welfare of the area is more likely to provide them with a job. Even tourism is seen as a dubious asset for an area by many. There are no easy answers to any of these conflicts, but teachers and pupils may need to define the environmental quality of life they want, before balancing it against other interests.

WHO SHOULD DECIDE?

With so many inherent clashes of interest over listed buildings, somebody has to decide between the competing claims, but it is hard to agree on a referee. Should decisions be made by the public or private sector, at a local or national level, by planners or architects, by experts or activists?

Most decisions are made at the local level. Planning offices, staffed by local government officers, advise elected councillors who make the decisions. Using qualified professionals who advise the decision makers who are in turn accountable to

Sun Street, Frome, has suffered from planning blight: these listed buildings, photographed in 1982, were compulsorily purchased by the Council in 1972 to make way for a ring road. In 1984 the road was cancelled, but the houses, empty for many years in the interim period, had deteriorated.

the public sounds like a good system, but it has its strains. Planners can be accused of being pressurized either by lack of time or by their political masters, or of being too obstructive to architects' innovative ideas. Councillors have been accused of favouring local commercial or prestigious schemes and of being too ignorant or too part-time to trust.

Some decisions are made at a national level. Independent planning inspectors preside over public inquiries, English Heritage officials give professional advice, and Parliament and the Secretary of State for the Environment can make important decisions. While people living locally to a dispute may question the right of people in London to make decisions about buildings remote from London, there are sometimes disagreements between civil servants and politicians. Recently English Heritage was in dispute with the sponsors of a parliamentary bill for the redevelopment of the King's Cross area of London. Clause 19 of this bill would have given the developers the right to set aside all listed building control in the area. This was a potentially disastrous precedent but English Heritage was prevented by the Court of Referees of the House of Commons from presenting its case to Parliament. Clause 19 was, however, then thrown out by a Commons Select Committee. Although politicians are accountable to their voters, and

despite the support that post-war governments have given to conservation, there can be no guarantee of consistent policy as the remarks from Macmillan and Wilson, already quoted, show.

Private developers and local amenity societies sometimes clash and sometimes co-operate over

treatment of listed buildings. Developers claim a part in decision making because they are often prepared to pay a lot of money towards conservation schemes and employ architects to draw up imaginative plans. Local amenity societies argue that they directly represent the people who will be affected by the developments. However, both groups have their critics who contend that developers are vulnerable to financial changes and responsible to distant investors, that architects are motivated by a desire to promote their personal reputations, and that amenity societies are amateurs promoting middle-class values, protecting the value of their own property, and holding to a not-in-my-back-yard philosophy.

All these groups, together with others, such as specialist-interest groups, housing associations and,

Station conversion was originally budgeted at £40 million, to come from private investment, but this figure rose to £230 million. English Heritage's income for 1990/91 was £90 million, of which £78 million came from the taxpayer. Such apparently enormous sums provoke questions: Who should pay for it all?

Who should choose how it's spent? Is it all worth it?

Conservationists, and most planners, are adamant that conservation is financially worthwhile. They argue that it is often cheaper to repair and adapt old buildings than it is to demolish, clear and rebuild. They point out

Air photograph of part of the King's Cross development area.

of course, the owners of listed buildings, combine to contest and co-operate over decisions about listed buildings. But when it comes to a conflict, who would you and your pupils like to see make the final decision?

MONEY

Conservation can be extremely expensive. The Battersea Power

Case study: Vale Royal House, Cheshire

Vale Royal, a Grade II listed building in Cheshire. It requires urgent repairs costing £1.5 million, but who should pay for them? Who is obliged to?

Vale Royal House in Cheshire is a Grade II listed building, a large country house whose heyday was between the wars. But since then it has decayed seriously and repairs to conserve it would now cost an estimated £1.5 million.

It's easy to say that the owners should pay for the repairs. But what if they can't? Vale Royal has only 25 acres and couldn't support the repair bill. What if the owners refuse to pay for repairs? For them, it may be financially worth letting the building fall down, so that the site can be redeveloped.

The local authority can allocate repair grants, or compulsorily purchase neglected buildings in order to preserve them. But is such expenditure of taxpayers' money justified? And what about the eight other big houses in the area with similar problems? Chester levied $1/2$ p per £1 on rates for conservation; how much would you be prepared to pay for conservation through

increased local taxes?

The Royal Commission has surveyed the building, and English Heritage does have money for historic buildings grants (£22.5 million in 1990/91), but cannot afford to pay for every deserving cause. In Vale Royal's case, a grant may be available for structural repairs if certain conditions are met. The private sector is often brought in to pay for conservation; with Vale Royal, developers are willing to find the £1.5 million needed, but they too set conditions: the two rival bids propose conversion to flats, or to a golf-club hotel. Both bids specify that a new housing development in the grounds, which would swamp the little village nearby, would be needed to finance the deal. And how far can the creation of a golf-course be said to 'preserve the setting' as the developers claim?

So - is it worth saving Vale Royal? If so, who pays, and who chooses how the money is spent?

that old buildings, especially stone ones, conserve heat more efficiently, and that old unique houses perform well on the housing market. The money spent on conservation is, in fact, modest when put against other expenditure: English Heritage's entire annual budget when it was set up was equivalent to the price of two yards of Falkland Islands runway! Though taxpayers may contribute £78 million a year to English Heritage, they contribute over £21 billion to defence.

THE CONTEXT

Listed buildings relate to their environmental context and can be adversely affected by changes to the surrounding areas. Views of St Paul's Cathedral have been obscured by the surrounding modern development. In Manchester, the destruction of Smithfield Market blighted many old buildings around it by destroying their physical setting and economic viability. On the other hand, should listed

Albert Embankment, London: the context of a conserved building is vital if it is not to appear ridiculous.

The tiny medal works photographed in 1956 has subsequently been demolished.

buildings be allowed to dominate their context?

One means of protecting the environmental context is the creation of Conservation Areas by local authorities under the 1967 Act, where whole areas are subject to much stricter planning controls. Alternatively, where streets or villages owe their attractive character not so much to buildings of individual merit but to the harmony created by a whole range or complex of buildings, the buildings may be listed for their group value.

WHAT SHOULD BE DONE WHEN THINGS GO WRONG?

Despite the controls, listed buildings do get destroyed, with or without permission. What punishments should we impose on owners who deliberately destroy their listed buildings? The Ancient Monuments Act of 1913 included hard labour and the cost of the repairs or rebuilding. Should we revive such penalties?

Both Church and Crown (government) property are exempt from listed building controls although the Church of England operates a separate system of controls. Some government properties, such as the Woolwich Arsenal, are in need of conservation work, but there is no legal way of making Government itself carry out such work.

So how should we control the controllers - the council or the government that allows decay, redevelopment or wholesale destruction? No.1 Poultry in London, widely believed to be a very important complex of buildings which should and could be saved, was, after a public inquiry, permitted by the then Secretary of State for the Environment Nicholas Ridley to be redeveloped. The organization SAVE took the matter to the High Court, and won a temporary reprieve for the buildings (later reversed by the Court of Appeal), but what can ordinary citizens in a democratic system do if they feel the wrong decision has been made? Lobby our representative politicians? Lie down in front of the bulldozers? Mobilize the power of the media?

In some cases, there is little that can be done once things have gone wrong, except to ensure that they

don't go wrong again. This involves as wide an awareness of the issues as possible, so education and the media have key roles. Involving pupils in such issues goes to the heart of educating them for their place in a democratic society.

Questions for discussion

■ What is the purpose of conserving anything old (especially buildings)?

■ What characteristics make a building worth conserving? Should we conserve buildings just because they are very old? What criteria should be used in judging a building to be architecturally or historically important?

■ When does the legal protection of buildings threaten the rights of owners to an unacceptable degree?

■ Can there be national rules deciding priorities (economy, traffic, heritage, etc.) for planners?

■ Who should make the final decision about the future of a listed building?

■ Who should pay for conservation of buildings? Should it be through increased local taxation?

■ What action is it acceptable and worthwhile for ordinary citizens to take in order to protect their local built environment?

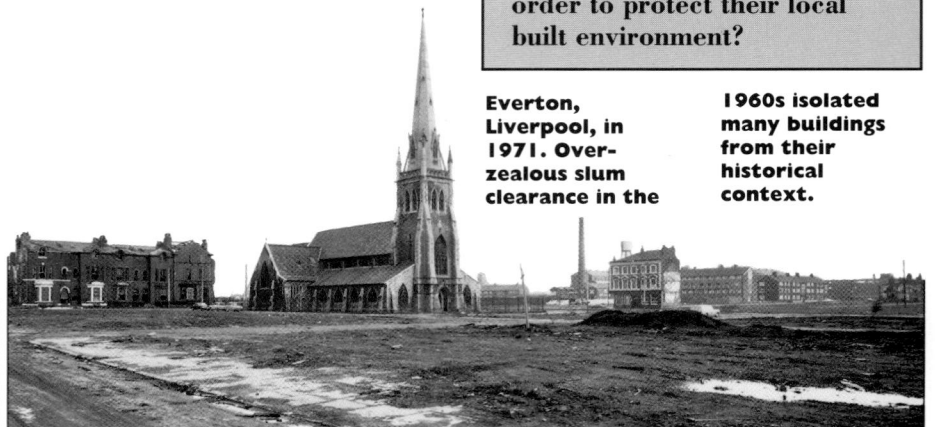

Everton, Liverpool, in 1971. Over-zealous slum clearance in the

1960s isolated many buildings from their historical context.

HOW TO INVOLVE PUPILS IN THE ISSUES

This chapter looks at some ways to prepare pupils in the classroom by making them more aware of listed buildings, their local environment and related issues. It suggests ways of identifying and becoming involved with local debates and gives ideas for fieldwork. Finally it suggests avenues for further research.

Before embarking on a topic on listed buildings define your educational objectives and intended outcomes. Decide what skills, concepts and knowledge you want your pupils to gain and how the work fits in with your curriculum. How will fieldwork fit in with preparation and follow-up? Most pupils will feel that they have achieved more if there is a tangible end-product. A slide programme, a video or an exhibition may document the whole process. Letters, articles and pictures in the press are exciting for pupils. A presentation, or simulated public inquiry, may be suitable to show to other classes, to parents, and perhaps to interested members of the public. Finally, you might try to get any original or researched material published by a local society.

CLASSROOM PREPARATION

Good preparation is essential to help avoid stereotyped or crude responses and to enable pupils to develop a point of view which they can sustain in debate. As well as introducing the facts and issues outlined earlier in this book you will also need to help your pupils become more sensitive to the built environment that surrounds them. You may like to try some of the following exercises.

Mental maps

Most people are remarkably unaware of their own environment, but don't realise it: they think that they have noticed everything, but in fact they have retained only a small, highly selective, proportion of what they see. To demonstrate this ask each pupil to draw as detailed a map as they can of their route to school, the immediate locality of the school or the local High Street, marking in as many of the

A mental map filled in by a year four pupil of Brighstone CE Primary School.

Mark in as many buildings as you can think of, in the right place on this map

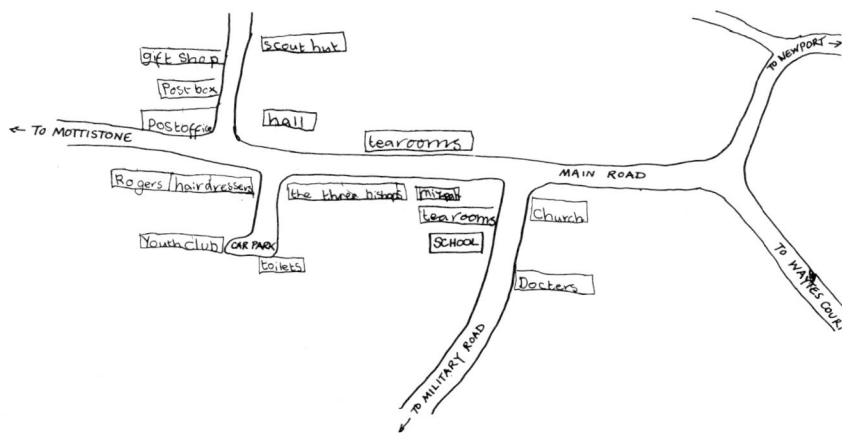

buildings as they can. Most pupils will chart very few buildings. A statistical survey of what was charted by pupils will also yield interesting results; some buildings will have been remembered by most pupils, and others by none. The class can then discuss why some buildings are more memorable than others.

Matching exercise

To help pupils learn what styles, features and functions are appropriate to specific types and ages of building, collect pictures of a variety of types of building and cut out specific features such as doors, windows or chimneys. The cut-out features should be jumbled up and displayed along with the buildings and the pupils then have to match each building with the correct features.

Grants simulation

Divide your class into groups and present them with the following fictitious problem:

Your group are the Trigport Council Planning Committee. You have been given £700,000 by a multi-millionaire who wishes to help his home town by paying for some repairs and restoration of old buildings. How are you going to split the money? You don't have to give money to all projects, or all the money that each is asking for. You may have to explain your choices to the Mayor (the teacher) and people of Trigport (the rest of the class). Trigport is a city of 200,000 inhabitants that would like to expand its tourism.

Eagle Thorpe Hall This fine nineteenth-century mansion is in urgent need of repairs, which would cost £1 million. A leisure company say that they will contribute £700,000 to convert it to a luxury hotel if the council can find the other £300,000. They say such a hotel is essential for Trigport's tourist prospects.

ELLA DORLEY-BROWN

No.8 Pitt Street This elegant but empty house, dated 1803, will need to be demolished if £70,000 cannot be found. The owners say that they have no money at all, but they are known to want to let the building fall down so that they can sell the site for redevelopment. Pitt Street is a road with many fine houses dated 1800 - 1810. A modern building might not fit in well.

The Cathedral The Cathedral is suffering from acid rain erosion (£2 million to repair), its spire is rapidly becoming unsafe (£6 million to repair) and the roof needs regilding inside (£200,000). Total bill: £8.2 million. The appeal fund has already raised £2.5 million but the trustees say that more money is needed for immediate urgent work. They point out that the Cathedral is Trigport's biggest tourist attraction.

The Wool House This ruin was once an important seventeenth-century house. The county's Historic Buildings Trust want to reconstruct it and use it as a heritage and information centre with a bookshop, a cafe and craft demonstrations. The work will cost £210,000.

Tow Farm Cottage This 1834 cottage is outside the town hidden away in a small valley. It is a perfectly-preserved example of a nineteenth-century farm labourer's dwelling. It is lived in by a near-penniless pensioner couple. It is in danger of falling down and needs £30,000 for urgent repairs.

Street Project Trigport's Conservation Area around the market place is looking a bit tatty. A project to smarten it up, by offering grants to the owners of the buildings for external minor repairs and for external repainting, would cost £150,000.

Railway Viaduct This twelve-arch span across the valley is a nationally important piece of early railway engineering. But since the railway has closed the viaduct has been crumbling and is now in a dangerous state. It would cost about £200,000 to demolish it and redevelop the area. It would cost £150,000 for immediate short-term repairs. Long-term repairs

would cost several million pounds.

Council Offices The building where your committee meets is shabby and uncomfortable. It is considered a disgraceful example of council sloppiness by members of the public who visit. £20,000 would make it smarter and more comfortable for you.

Each group should have time to arrive at an agreed distribution of the money. The groups should then present their solutions which can be compared on the blackboard. The solutions should be justified by each group, and then discussed.

The issues that will emerge in discussions will be wide. Should grants aid commercial enterprises? Should owners be forced to conserve? What happens when owners have inadequate financial resources? Should gentrification be supported? Should grants be given for social or emotional reasons? Should large or small projects be attempted? Should buildings not seen or used by the public be supported? How important is the historic heritage? Should solutions be short- or long-term? Should grants be conditional on owners' promises? How can you justify subjective decisions? What is the aim of conservation grants?

Getting the message

Every building says something about the people who commissioned it, built it, designed it, lived in it and/or maintained it. Sometimes the message is a subtle one but often a very deliberate statement is made. The Hoover Factory, built in London in the inter-war years and now listed, was intended to give Hoover a glamorous modern image: it resembled a Hollywood palace set in a garden. Older pupils might collect pictures of buildings and start to analyse the message being delivered. Younger pupils could look at some pictures or local examples of buildings with very clear messages (e.g. vast, impressive palace, solid town hall, Victorian prison, utilitarian office block) and then be asked to design a building that reflected the desired image of an organisation or product. The task will be easier and more productive if you give your pupils a very specific brief.

ROYAL COMMISSION ON THE HISTORICAL BUILDINGS OF ENGLAND

GETTING INVOLVED IN THE LOCAL ISSUES

An issues-based approach to listed buildings will generate the need for further research, and to sharpen the focus and stimulate involvement pupils should be encouraged to find out as much as possible for themselves.

The local planning office will hold a copy of the list of historic buildings for the area and is also the obvious place to start to find out about current local issues. Some county planning offices, like Derbyshire, have an officer with responsibility for education, and some, like Hampshire, publish information especially for teachers. By law, all citizens have the right to go to the local planning office and look at any plans for their neighbourhood. Notices of changes should be posted at the site concerned, and announcements about the changes published in the local papers, so that objections can be lodged.

Another starting point may be to monitor the national and local media, and to display articles and notices of Listed Building Consent on a class notice-board. Older pupils may be able to contribute the majority of the clippings once the project is under way. However, to involve all the pupils the teacher will have to draw the class's attention to the boards and highlight the developments regularly. The need to encourage involvement must be balanced by the need to avoid prejudices forming.

Once the local issues have emerged try to involve people from outside the school. Invite local planners, journalists, local politicians, and amenity society campaigners to give their point of view. Hold a preparatory session to encourage pupils to formulate suitable questions and brief visitors carefully on what to expect or what is expected from them. If the speaker agrees, consider recording as much as possible on tape.

Once the relevant facts have been gathered, the issues should be clearly identified and discussed. What are the alternative solutions? What are the costs and who is making decisions? What conflicts of interest and ideas are there? A role play exercise based on submissions to a public inquiry is a good way to stimulate involvement, clarify issues and identify solutions. Groups of pupils can be asked to argue the cases of different interest groups. The example given here is based on Ryde Pavilion but you will probably be able to develop a similar exercise round a local case where fieldwork would be an essential part of research.

ISLE OF WIGHT COUNTY PRESS

The Hoover Factory, Western Avenue, Ealing. Grade II* listed building.

Local people protesting against plans to develop Ryde Pavilion.

Ryde Pavilion public inquiry

Read and discuss the Ryde documents and clippings. The local issues should be clarified, as necessary. Teaching staff or older pupils could take on the role of interested parties and be interviewed by pupils. Explain the purpose of a public inquiry and show pupils how they might make use of some of the issues raised earlier in this book in putting their case. Split your pupils into groups with each group assigned to a role.

The group roles

■ **Water Planet Limited.** See documents 1, 5. This group must persuade the inquiry that they are a reputable company with exciting proposals that will benefit Ryde.

■ **Medina Borough Council.** See documents 1, 2, 5. This group must persuade that they are democratically elected to look after the economic and environmental interests of Ryde, and that COPAS are a minority.

ISLE OF WIGHT COUNTY PRESS — FRIDAY, NOVEMBER 17, 1989

BATTLE OVER RYDE PAVILION

②

Mick Jagger's support sought for campaign

By CLIVE BARTON

A YOUNG Mick Jagger performing at Ryde pavilion in the sixties sang I Can't Get No Satisfaction. Now the millionaire Rolling Stone will be invited to express virtually the same sentiment on behalf of the COPAS group trying to save the building.

The Stones' management was being contacted this week asking Jagger, and possibly other members of the group, to raise their voices on behalf of this early scene of their success.

It is the latest twist to a saga which has now seen a hate campaign launched against Mr.

John Ritchie, Medina's mayor.

In addition, there is the formation of an opposing knock it down body keen to see Water Planet develop the site.

Both groups say they are happy to let a public referendum decide, but Mr. Ritchie is adamant that the borough council needs no such sanction.

Against this background, experts from English Heritage were due to inspect the building yesterday.

COPAS has hinted that it would end its occupation of the pavilion once the inspection was completed, but members believed Medina would block yesterday's visit by refusing English Heritage entry to the pavilion on the grounds that the building was unsafe.

COPAS backed the approach to the Stones at the suggestion of one of its supporters, Mr. Geoff Francis.

A worrying feature of the argument, which both sides say they deplore, is the appearance of dozens of yellow stickers in the town circulated by Vectis Volunteers For Vengeance.

These attack Medina council in general and Mr. Ritchie in particular, including such phrases as Ritchie Is A Rotter and giving his phone number at Ryde.

When informed of this on Monday, Mr. Ritchie told the County Press, "It is horrifying to think I have become a personal target.

"It is all very well for COPAS to say it is nothing to do with it, but I don't accept that. This whole thing has been steadily escalated by them and now some of the wilder fringes are going completely over the top!"

That day, the council sent COPAS' solicitors a letter instructing the rooftop protesters to leave by noon the following day, or otherwise expect a county court writ ordering them to do so — plus the bill for costs.

Miss Jose Wellspring, a leading member, told the CP, "Our solicitors replied immediately that this was an unreasonable demand, giving inadequate time.

"They asked that the matter be held in abeyance until Thursday so that they could take instructions."

She explained that this would enable English Heritage, which advises the Department of the Environment, to make an impartial inspection which COPAS was convinced would strengthen its case.

"Frankly we don't trust Medina," she said.

"We've seen the sort of vandalism it did to one of the turrets the other day, and we're determined to stop it doing any more."

Mr. Barry Leadbetter, the council's leisure and development manager, said, "That's nonsense! The building was listed by the DoE, and we certainly wouldn't flout that order!"

However, he was officially questioning the listing, warning that the council might seek a judicial ruling.

Mr. Ian Morgan, council leader, said it was clear that COPAS, although including some genuine protesters, had some nasty types in its ranks.

Group horrified at £2.5m Water Planet idea

①

RYDE SEAFRONT PLAN UNDER FIRE

By CLIVE BARTON

RESISTANCE is already mounting in Ryde to Medina councillors' initial blessing for a £2.5m plan to replace the Esplanade Pavilion with a Water Planet — a two-storey building on a marine theme.

When the amenities and tourism committee last week unanimously backed the scheme in principle, members agreed to hold a public presentation at Ryde Town Hall on Monday to test local opinion.

Already, however, the Green Party has condemned the scheme, a nearby hotelier has expressed fears, and a shock wave has gone through the 2,000-strong Conserve Our Pavilion and Seafront group.

Mr. Norman Bartholomew, chairman of the Ryde Eastern Gardens Working Party, which urged the committee to give initial backing, described the idea as marvellous.

He said, "We will be replacing the pavilion for the people of Ryde. I know there has been argument about doing the place up, and we considered that, but it is in a very poor state of repair."

Mr. Ian Morgan, council leader, said the project was exciting. "It should certainly put Ryde and the IW on the map."

Mr. David Icke, the Greens' prospective Parliamentary candidate for the Island, held the opposite view.

"Many people will be taken aback after being told that demolition of the pavilion was no part of Medina's plans," he said.

"It is all very well to say there will be a public presentation, but why was there no pre-consultation?

"We must remember we are talking about one of the two great landmarks in Ryde, and it shouldn't be treated in such a cavalier fashion.

"It is pretty rich, to say the least, for councillors to claim the pavilion is in a bad state when they are the ones responsible.

"We also need to know far more about the company behind the scheme."

Co-director of Water Planet Ltd, a newly-formed organisation at Christchurch, Dorset, are Mr. Timothy Rusby and Mr. Stuart Beavan.

Mr. Rusby said they had plans for seven water theme centres nationwide. Ryde's looked set to be the first, in view of the warm response they had received when replying to the borough council's advertisement for entrepreneurs to develop the seafront.

"Right from the word go the councillors were enthusiastic," he said. "Our plan is unlike any other in the Island and the whole county could benefit."

Mr. Rusby said the intention was a multi-functional centre in landscaped grounds, with room for 250 diners or 400 disco dancers.

A special feature would be a mock-up of the Beagle, the ship in which Darwin voyaged, which would appear to float in a harbour setting enhanced by tanks of tropical and native fish.

"It could provide 30 to 40 jobs and be an all-year-round attraction," he added. "If everything works out, we could be operating by Whitsun, 1990."

He emphasised that there was no intention to encroach on to the bowling greens area, and said the aim was to submit a planning application before the end of July.

Mr. Geoff Watts, owner of the Dean House Hotel in Dover Street, overlooking the site, thought it an entirely unsuitable project which would rob Ryde of one of its most important and popular buildings.

"The sort of attractions they seem to be planning are already well catered for by the two Warner camps not far away," said Mr. Watts.

"We seem to be trying to copy the pleasure parks ideas of Southsea when we really need upmarket facilities in keeping with the atmosphere of the town.

"Maybe a conference centre and facilities like indoor bowls or other sports would be all right. At least parts of the present pavilion should be maintained to retain the traditional character."

Mr. Peter Cradock, chairman of the Conserve Our Pavilion and Seafront group, said it was extraordinary that the council seemed determined to dispose of the building despite all the pleas for its retention and suggestions for alternative uses.

"They talk about an all-year-round attraction, but the majority of residents in the town are over 55 and I can't see them taking to disco dancing," he said.

"My group will have to consider the facts when more detail is known, but my initial reaction, and that of members I have spoken to, is one of horror."

The public meeting at which the plans will be displayed is being held at Ryde Town Hall on Monday.

This is an artist's impression of the development given initial backing by Medina councillors, but modifications are expected before they are revealed at Monday's public presentation.

Counter protest group wants pavilion to go

③

THE Ryde Pavilion saga took another dramatic new twist this week with the formation of a group in favour of the distinctive building's re-development.

ROPAMA — Replace Our Pavilion And Move Ahead — has been formed in direct opposition to COPAS — Conserve Our Pavilion And Seafront — to support the Water Planet concept advocated by Medina Borough Council.

The new group, though barely a week old, has already gathered scores of supporters and membership was growing by the day, said founder Mrs. Angela Reed, of the Melville Hotel, Ryde.

"We want to show the council and the Water Planet company that there is a lot of support in the town for the development," she said.

Many objectors to the Water Planet concept had been misinformed and had not realised that the plans include provision for improved theatre facilities, she claimed.

"It is sad we are in danger of letting the chance of the town getting a first-class theatre slip through our fingers because of this misinformation."

Mrs. Reed said Chichester-based Water Planet had confirmed the new theatre scheme would have a maximum seating capacity of 440, in comparison to the pavilion's 220.

She is convinced that ROPAMA represents the majority view of Ryde people and backs the idea of a referendum to decide the issue.

A petition calling for the scheme to go ahead is in circulation in the town and has been signed by several hundred people.

"The fact is that the current theatre is pretty grotty and here is a chance to get better facilities which would attract bigger acts and bring more business to the town," said Mrs. Reed.

"I am not a member of any political party, my interest is that of a ratepayer who wants the best deal for Ryde."

Mr. Ian Morgan, leader of Medina Borough Council, has welcomed ROPAMA.

"I think people have become fed up with a vociferous few gaining all the headlines," he said.

● For latest legal moves over Ryde Pavilion see page 2.

■ **COPAS group (Conserve Our Pavilion And Seafront). See documents 1, 2, 4, 6, 8, 9, 10.** This group must persuade the inquiry that the Pavilion, a 1920s sea-front theatre, is worth keeping, that the Water Planet shouldn't be built in Ryde, and that the Council is wrong.

■ **ROPAMA group (Replace Our Pavilion And Move Ahead). See documents 1, 3, 8.** This group must persuade the inquiry that ordinary locals want the new building and that Ryde's future is better with change.

■ **English Heritage. See documents 2, 5.** This group must persuade that the Pavilion is worth keeping for architectural or historical reasons.

■ **Architects.** Produce plans to show how the Pavilion could be restored, or ideas on how to adapt it for new functions that would enhance its role.

■ **The media team.** Newspaper articles and/or a video news item covering the story.

■ **The inquiry chairperson.** To chair the inquiry (probably the teacher).

Groups can then research arguments, write a speech for the inquiry, set out a visual presentation to support the case, design or devise an accompanying campaign of action, liaise with other groups, and plan interviews with the media. The public inquiry is held, and a decision taken. A plan of action is agreed on based on the findings of the public inquiry.

200 in seafront demo to defend Ryde Pavilion

BANNER-waving campaigners turned out in force at Ryde Esplanade Pavilion on Monday to show the strength of opposition to plans to demolish the building.

At one point more than 200 local residents demonstrating against Medina's controversial decision to send in the bulldozers linked arms round the theatre, creating a human chain.

Despite a small outburst when a Medina Borough Council supervisor ripped down a protest banner from the outside of the building, the non-political demonstration went ahead without a hitch.

"I'm very impressed with the turnout," said Miss Jose Wellspring, president of the Conserve Our Pavilion And Seafront (COPAS) group.

This demonstration has come about in just four days — it's wonderful that so many have come along."

Mrs. Dorothy Key, of Haylands, one of the under-members of COPAS, echoed the views of protesters. "I remember seeing this pavilion built and I think what the council is doing is disgraceful," she said.

"I hope this protest will work — it should have been made a long time ago."

Many who had turned up in support were members of local theatre companies which have used the building over the years.

Mrs. Mary Anderson, principal of the Appley Stage School, said that all who had used the pavilion were very fond of it.

"As a small theatre group we could not afford to hire this hall," she said. "There's no way we will be able to afford to go elsewhere. We are all very proud of this building — it's the pride of Ryde."

To those involved with the IW Musical Competition Festival, the loss of the principal dancing and drama venue is more than a disappointment.

"I don't know what we will do this year without the pavilion," said a festival committee spokesperson. "There are so many elderly people from the Ryde area who came here year after year. Where are they going to go?

"This is our jubilee year and we booked this theatre at the close of last year's competition. We weren't told anything. All the council's proposals have been very underhand."

Youngsters opposing the demolition gave up the first morning of their half-term holiday to support COPAS members.

Katie and Joanne Walls and friend Lindsay Smith, all pupils at Swanmore Middle School, are in agreement that the Water Planet scheme should not be allowed.

"We don't want to see the pavilion go," said Lindsay, nine.

According to one local resident, COPAS member Mr. David Burnett, the public protest had proved to the council that it was not just a minority group in favour of keeping the pavilion.

It will not be known until the end of the week whether a second plea to the Department of the Environment could win an 11th-hour reprieve for the building.

Meanwhile, Ryde residents hope this first public protest will help their fight.

"It could have an effect, if there's any democracy in the world," said local man Mr. John McGee.

See page 46 for details of the latest move in Ryde's fight to keep the pavilion open.

⑤ Building dangerous warns Medina

THE Department of the Environment was wrong to list the pavilion as a building of architectural merit, Medina council claimed in a statement this week.

Medina said a dangerous building had been listed without the opportunity of putting the view reflected by the majority of the community.

"At no time has the council issued any order for the demolition of the pavilion — merely to carry out works to ascertain the condition of the building as requested by the minister," the statement said.

"We have requested that COPAS ends its illegal occupation of the building to enable investigations to be completed and make the building safe for the protection of the public. It must be remembered that this building is subject to a dangerous building notice.

● Water Planet now regrets its choice of Ryde as the first place to launch its pilot project.

Mr. Tim Rushby, director, told the County Press, "We want to build a number of these centres, but in retrospect, we might have had a much easier time by starting somewhere else.

"I suppose the fact is, the Island has had such a raw deal from some mainland developers that its hypersensitive these days."

Nevertheless, his firm remained committed to the £2.5 million complex, convinced that the Environment Department's listing of the building was only a short-term measure.

● Everything from tea and coffee to champagne, hot sausage rolls to boxes of chocolates, and a vast supply of blankets have been donated to the grateful COPAS members who have been on the pavilion site for a week.

⑥ Pavilion clash just symptom of more dangerous disease

THE latest clash between the council and COPAS protesters represents a local matter, which unfortunately goes deeper and has wider implications on a national level.

The recent events at Ryde Pavilion illustrates a situation that has become endemic in this country, whereby political authorities (the Government, Parliament, local government, etc.) are at best riding roughshod over the wishes and liberties of their electors and at worst are deliberately ignoring democratic procedures.

This has been evident in water metering, the ambulancemen's dispute, the National Health Service, etc. This ignoring of the electors' wishes has been highlighted on a local level by the conflict over the pavilion.

Unfortunately big business, egged on by its illegitimate sons greed and speculation, is leading our councillors and politicians by the nose right up the path of short-term gain.

Listen to councillors squeal as Whitbread Plc leans on them and applies pressure! The result? Down comes one of the oldest, most historically interesting buildings in Ryde — the Prince of Wales pub. Round of applause for the councillors! Why? you ask! Because this very building was in the Ryde conservation area. It takes quite some barefaced, short-sighted, ignorant double-dealing to achieve that.

Now with another large company (and this one is a property developer — always good for a bit of urban and rural rape) breathing down its necks and leaning heavily on the council's soft, feeble underbelly, the Medina Borough Council is wholeheartedly playing sit-up-and-beg lapdog to the new gods of progress, the saviours of our Island — property speculators!

All hail to the new Messiahs promising salvation through new modern, mainland-style, large-scale leisure complex developments! Short-term gain rears its lucrative head again!

Yes, now it's the turn of the Ryde Pavilion. But what is happening at the pavilion is only a symptom of a more insidious, more dangerous, all-embracing disease that is national in character, not only local.

Authorities, ignoring the wishes of its electors, blunder blindly and pig-headedly towards an objective which they will pursue no matter what in the interests of commercial short-term gain. It is a problem that manifests itself at Ryde in the conflict between heritage conservationists and commercial speculation.

On a national level, it is seen in the conflict between ambulancemen and the National Health Executive, with the Government refusing to go to independent arbitration.

R. S. J. MARTIN,
71 Marlborough Road
Elmfield, Ryde

⑦ Minority jeopardise future prosperity

I LIKE many others in Ryde have been concerned that the coverage that the COPAS group has received has given a false impression with regard to the wishes of Ryde people.

The majority wish to see the pavilion replaced with the proposed Water Planet/theatre complex which would serve a wider range of people young and old alike and not be a continual burden on our rates.

It seems inconceivable that a building which is only 63 years old (not Victorian) which has three times been refused listed building status should be saved at the future cost of our younger generation.

As well as the Water Planet concept the development provides a theatre with seating for up to 630 people. The three dressing rooms all provide en-suite facilities which anyone who has used the pavilion's facilities would surely welcome.

Fire regulations restrict the existing pavilion to a limit of approximately 220 people.

As a result of my concern I have formed a group called ROPAMA — Replace Our Pavilion and Move Ahead.

Although the people of Ryde gave the council a two-to-one mandate to replace the pavilion, a minority group could jeopardise Ryde's future prosperity.

Please contact ROPAMA on IW 63444.

A. P. REED (Mrs.)
Melville Hotel
29 Melville Street, Ryde

⑧ Westridge a more fitting site for concrete edifice

I HAVE the greatest admiration for the sensitive, foresighted people who are protecting our pavilion from demolition.

Often featured in postcards and brochures the pavilion is, I believe, the part of Ryde that her exiles dream of. It epitomises Ryde, with its gentle Victorian and Edwardian environs — so beautifully enhanced this summer with outstanding floral displays.

Surely it is time Medina Borough Council faced up to the fact that it is not owners, but custodians of our heritage; charged, like it or not, with duties to protect and maintain it, while providing for the needs of our young.

If it is to banish its present image of foolhardy philistines it will have to learn the art of balancing these legitimate requirements effectively.

The Tesco superstore was built with the proviso that the people of Ryde should be treated to various sports amenities at the Westridge Centre which has since been closed.

Now we hear tell that Leading Leisure may not be providing the improved facilities it offered for the privilege of building its holiday village there.

So maybe the Water Planet developer should consider trying to acquire part of this site for its concrete edifice — where it would be equally accessible and architecturally more fitting?

PAULINE HUNTER
2 Arnold Road, Binstead

⑨ Protesters preventing bulldozer 'accident'

FROM all the evidence I have seen, it would seem Medina Borough Council is hell-bent on re-developing (demolishing) the Ryde Pavilion and it is no wonder COPAS members don't trust it.

So far the council has displayed a pretty good record for underhanded machinations.

The council is itching to get its sticky, money-soiled hands on that site but a nice levelled site is strongly preferable.

We are told over 5,000 have signed a petition against re-development of the pavilion. This is no small number and represents a large significant percentage of population, especially if one takes into account a large number of the silent majority, like myself, who firmly support COPAS but have not signed or made their voices heard due, unfortunately to laziness.

But this large significant consensus of support for the pavilion is being "democratically" ignored by our council elected to work and serve its electors.

The mayor resorts to a tired old cliche, much frequented

by tyrants when backed into a corner by people fighting for common justice. This paints the opposition leaders as evil, ignorant or foolish and suggests their followers are suspect people, often on the margin of society being led by a group of fanatical misguided Machiavellian agitators.

Noting could be further from the truth, if one looks at the peaceful and reasonable manner in which COPAS has behaved.

In fact, ironically, "nasty, outrageous people, foolishly led" could serve as a good description of our council and mayor.

Surely the most naive, or publicly naive, statement award goes to Mr. Ian Morgan who said that because of the injunction and listing COPAS was wasting its time on the roof suggesting there was no need for a 24-hour vigil.

But Mr. Morgan, surely you know that one well placed bulldozer, driven by one conveniently mis-informed driver, does wonders for stubborn buildings that refuse to come down?

S. WHEELER
19 Station Avenue
Sandown

⑩ No such democracy now

WHEN Ryde Pavilion was built in the twenties, all local ratepayers were asked to vote and 75 percent voted for it.

Where is such simple democracy today? Ratepayers have not been asked if they want to keep the pavilion. Nor have they been asked if they want a gigantic car park on Ryde sands, which is part and parcel of the package deal.

The few people who were aware of the questionnaire on the Water Planet project were asked if such a new building was a good idea. No mention of pulling down the pavilion,

despite the fact that a reappraisal of the listing of the pavilion was underway.

COPAS is prepared to spend its own trust fund money to preserve the building and to restore the pavilion to its old glory. The cost is nowhere near the amount being suggested and the burden is not intended to come on the local rates.

The pavilion does draw the summer crowds. Can the same be said for a glorified fish tank?

C. A. E. ARNOLD
10 Woodlands Close, Ryde

If you have managed to select a local problem then with careful preparation any discussion, role play or mock public inquiry will result in pupils having informed opinions of their own about what the local solutions of the conflict should be. The next stage of the discussion should be to debate what the pupils should and can do about it. A plan of action should be drawn up and put into effect. Depending on the case, some of the following may be appropriate: writing letters to the press, lobbying those who take the relevant decisions, carrying out a survey (of opinions, traffic flow, etc.) or extra research to prove a point or find out more, offering to help with restoration work, or inviting journalists to cover some staged event. For instance, Ilfracombe School's pupils manufactured reproduction Victorian letter tiles that replaced missing ones around their town.

Portsea Workhouse

Two Portsmouth schools, Crookhorn School and Isambard Middle School, together with Southampton University, have made a rewarding study of the Grade II listed Portsea Workhouse. The demolition of this example of Victorian architecture and social history was favoured by the city council and the regional health authority in order to make room for the expansion of St Mary's Hospital. Conservation groups, including the Victorian Society, the Hampshire Field Club and the Portsmouth Society, campaigned against demolition. In the ensuing war of words, the two schools' involvement included historical documentary research, fieldwork, oral history, and active lobbying to save the building. Pupils took part in a simulated public inquiry, taking roles, and some attended the real public inquiry, where their teacher spoke for their point of view. The building has now been saved, and Portsmouth Building Association are converting it to housing for the homeless. One of the possible reasons for the government inspector who presided over the public inquiry recommending the conservation of the workhouse may well have been its educational value. Southampton University has produced an extensive education pack based on the story.

'PLEASE SAVE WORKHOUSE'

Schoolchildren in rescue campaign

...at a Portsmouth school today mounted their own...save the city's old workhouse.

...l-year-olds in Mrs. Jennifer Shutler's third-year...school has written a letter to City Planning...council not to back proposals to pull down...

...the area," Mrs...gained... of re...It

By GIE BEDDOES

THE NEWS, FRIDAY, JANUARY 30, 1987—17

Poor house gives pupils rich lesson

PILS from Crookhorn School, Purbrook, and staff from ...mpton University have joined the campaign to save Portsmouth's ...ent early Victorian workhouse, near St Mary's Hospital, after ...e building as part of a new G.C.S.E. history course.

...f about 20 pupils visited the workhouse at St Mary's Road, to take ...Archaeology and Education project designed by Southampton ...funded by the Manpower Services Commission.

By MARGARET WEST

...ing their
...Peter
...rofes-
...at
...of
...rt-

...of the Southampton project.

She said: "It is the only remaining example of a building designed jointly by the architect Augustus ...vesay and Thomas ...en.

...he shell is remarkably ...d and the pupils were ...go in and make a ...the conditions of ...19th Century.

...oper said the ...roject had been ...designed to show pupils the stark contrast between the elegant, Italianate facade of the building, and the grim conditions inside where the paupers slept in crowded dormitories in 2ft. 3in. wide beds with only 1ft. 3in. between the beds.

Children slept in twos in 4ft. wide beds, and were hired out to farmers in little gangs to work in the fields.

Adults performed soul-destroying tasks such as bone crushing, flint breaking and picking Oakum — unravelling old rope for re-cycling.

Mrs. Cooper said the workhouse was in an invaluable aid to studying the Victorian Poor Law. "Our pupils were shocked to see how families were divided at the Porter's Lodge, the males going to one wing and the females to another, perhaps never to meet again."

The boardroom with its superb pine panelling, stained glass, moulded cornice and marble fireplace was still in very good condition and worth retaining.

Mrs. Cooper said the children and their parents planned to write to the Wessex Health Authority asking it to find a compromise way of extending St Mary's Hospital without knocking the main building down.

Mr. Peter Stone, Manager of the university project, said: "We would like the main building retained. We want to set up an educational resource on the workhouse for use by other Portsmouth area schools."

Campaigners from Isambard Middle School outside St Mary's House Portsmouth today. — Photo sales no. 5047-1

Workhouse days recalled

HISTORY came alive for senior pupils at Crookhorn School, Purbrook, when two elderly sisters recalled what it was like to grow up as inmates of Portsmouth's historic workhouse.

The magnificent early Victorian workhouse, now under threat of redevelopment, is being studied by Crookhorn pupils as part of their G.C.S.E. history course.

They have already visited the building to see for themselves how grim conditions were for the early residents under the Poor Law, despite the elegant Italianate facade.

As a result of an appeal in The News, two sisters, Mrs. Mary Johnson (66), of Chichester, and Miss Annie Barnett (74), of Lee-on-Solent, offered to answer pupils' questions about their early lives in the workhouse.

Fourth and fifth year pupils heard them describe their childhood under a regime almost as strict as when the workhouse was founded in 1845.

The sisters came from a Portsea family of five children, three of whom died of poverty and disease. "If we had not gone into the workhouse we would not have survived," said Mrs. Johnson.

"Father was in the dockyard, and he was dismissed when the men came back from the First World War. We had no money to buy food or pay the rent. Mother was very bitter about it, but father was different. As long as he had his clay pipe to smoke he was happy."

Miss Barnett said that tobacco was eight old pence an ounce, and beer was even cheaper. Neither sister recalled having any possessions or toys while at home or in the workhouse.

Crookhorn's Pastoral Co-ordinator Mrs. Pam Cooper, said: "We hope to speak at the public inquiry into plans to demolish the workhouse. Pupils realize that St Mary's Hospital does need space to expand, but we will ask for the shell of the workhouse to be kept, as it is of such great historical and architectural importance to the city."

● Crookhorn pupils Susan Legg (left) and Samantha Thornton, both aged 14, are pictured discussing the future of the Portsea workhouse with Miss Barnett (left) and Mrs. Johnson
— Photo sales no. 0529-1

● The impressive facade of the workhouse which hid the grim facts of life inside.

FIELDWORK

Pupils will not learn about building conservation solely through classroom activities and a fieldwork programme needs to be an integral part of the process.

Practicalities

The owners of buildings to be visited should always be consulted. Many will be only too pleased to show round reasonably-sized parties and to talk about the building. They may be able to lend old pictures or documents connected with the building. Other people may be invaluable in accompanying visits: planners, locals with long memories, and others who can inform pupils.

On the other hand, some owners of listed buildings may not be pleased by the attention of schools, and some buildings may be in an unsafe condition: in such cases it is obviously advisable to limit fieldwork to studying from an acceptable distance or to change the plans.

Priming pupils will vary according to the nature of the visit. Often pupils will need the historical, social and geographical context before they can fully understand the significance of what they are looking at. Reading extracts from an appropriate historical novel can spark pupils' imagination. They will certainly need to understand all the technical, architectural and historical terms that they might encounter in their fieldwork. Their fieldwork skills can also be sharpened beforehand with observational and recording games and exercises. The sites of listed buildings often involve hazards such as traffic and they may not have essentials like lavatories nearby. You will need to survey the site before a visit to check that there are safe dry vantage points for pupils to stand or sit when doing their fieldwork. If appropriate, you should also try out any activity sheet to check its feasibility, and warn local inhabitants of the visit. The ideas that follow show some approaches that could be adapted to a variety of buildings and environments.

The walk

A walk around the local buildings is the obvious follow-up to the mental maps exercise to check what was or wasn't remembered. It is also the obvious introduction to issues of change in buildings and conservation. Your pupils will need a clear idea of the aims of the visit and must have specific things to do, see or note. It may be well worth the teacher making a checklist for pupils to fill in. Below are some suggestions for aspects on which to focus observations; it is unlikely to be worth taking more than two aspects at a time.

■ Ask pupils to note which buildings they find interesting and to say why. This can be compared with the buildings they remembered for their mental maps.

■ Ask pupils to note which buildings are the oldest. What are the common features that identify old buildings (styles, materials, size, etc.)?

■ Ask pupils to identify new buildings which are decorated to look old. Look for fake leaded windows, new coach lamps, half-timbered integral garages, neo-Georgian bow windows, Tudor lettering and spelling, etc.

■ Ask pupils to look for changes to buildings. Identify replacement windows, extensions, blocked doors and windows, new roofing, etc. This approach can be followed by discussion as to why people want these changes.

■ Ask pupils to look for clues that tell them something about the owners or occupiers of the building. Are they rich/poor, young/old? What interests do they have? What do names tell us? Is the business prosperous or not? What image is being projected?

■ Ask pupils to note building materials. This can be followed up with questions about which materials are local, are natural or artificial, are used for old or new buildings.

■ Ask pupils to note visible examples of building conservation, or buildings in need of conservation.

■ Ask pupils to note their sensory perceptions around buildings: sounds, smells, touch, and feelings about buildings. Responses can be stimulated by asking pupils to vary their pace, by getting closer or further away from the buildings, or by shutting out one or more of their senses.

Careful observation of change.

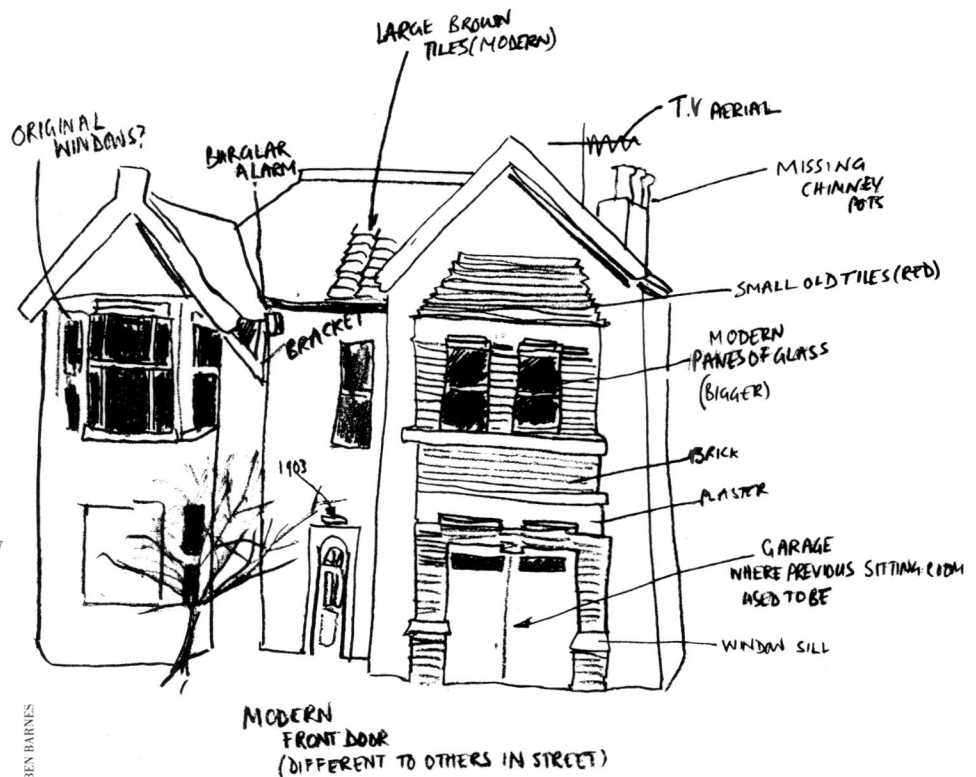

LARGE BROWN TILES (MODERN)

ORIGINAL WINDOWS?

BURGLAR ALARM

BRACKET

1903

MODERN FRONT DOOR (DIFFERENT TO OTHERS IN STREET)

T.V AERIAL

MISSING CHIMNEY POTS

SMALL OLD TILES (RED)

MODERN PANES OF GLASS (BIGGER)

BRICK

PLASTER

GARAGE WHERE PREVIOUS SITTING ROOM USED TO BE

WINDOW SILL

BEN BARNES

DAVID JONES

Encourage pupils to distinguish between a specific style and a revival of that style. Cheam, Surrey.

With any of these approaches, it is important to allow time for pupils to pursue their particular interest: many of them will be able to contribute anecdotes or historical information about local buildings. Equally, it is important to allow class time for discussion of the results of the walks survey.

Slide programme

The local walk can be used to generate a slide programme that focuses on specific aspects of the locality. This is most useful if it is produced by the pupils themselves. It will involve them in defining the topic, planning the shots, photographing, editing, producing a commentary that fits both the pictures and the topic/idea, operating slide projectors and tape-recorders, speaking clearly, and evaluating the finished product. The topic focus will vary according to the locality and pupils' ages, but may involve identifying buildings worth conserving or converting, or how the area is changing. If the production of a slide programme is too difficult, pupils could produce a story board with Polaroid photographs instead.

Five photos exercise

The criteria for listing buildings are that they should be of special architectural or historical interest. Split the class into groups and provide each group with a camera. Ask each group to identify five local buildings that best fit the criteria for listing, and to photograph each

A group of Medina High School pupils' personal choice of the five most important buildings to conserve in Newport, Isle of Wight.

building to illustrate its age or interest. The photographs of each group can be displayed and compared, with each group having to justify its choices to the other groups.

This activity can be developed to fit local circumstances and the abilities and interests of the class. Alternative tasks could be the selection of the five buildings most in need of conservation work, the five buildings most suitable for conversion to another function, five views that show buildings of group value, or the five modern buildings most deserving of listing in the future. The important thing is for pupils to argue their choices, both within their group and to the other group, and to base their arguments on what they have seen.

Angles

This exercise helps set an individual building in its context. The building is sketched or photographed from as many different angles and vantage points as possible, at varying ranges. Display the results back at school and draw conclusions. Which view shows the building at its best, and why? Does the building 'fit in' from all or just some angles? Is it older/newer than the buildings that surround it? Do the sides and rear of the building reveal more about its function and history than the front? What can be deduced about the interior from the exterior?

Questions about the historical and geographical context will follow logically: Has the building been influenced by the buildings around it? Are there signs of changes of use? How has it been influenced by its geographical context?

Observation game

A game to start a fieldwork session on an individual listed building which will get the pupils looking carefully for details involves the group looking at the building and each pupil in turn naming a feature he or she can see. No one is allowed to repeat a feature, and if they cannot name a new feature, they are eliminated. The last person in is the winner.

Drawing

One of the best ways of fostering a really detailed scrutiny of a local

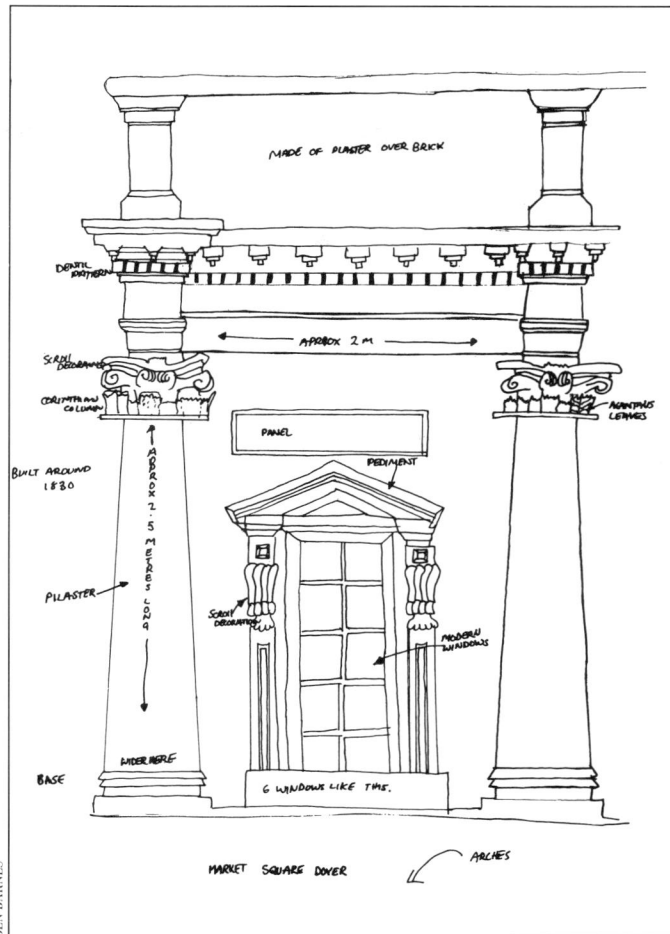

A window from Dover Museum.

Thick felt tips or wax crayons will help pupils produce bold drawings.

building is to set pupils to draw it. The activity slows them down and engages the eye with the building. Older pupils may have become self-conscious about their drawing skills but stress to them that the purpose of the activity is to make a record rather than to produce a work of art. Encourage pupils to label their drawings using any technical vocabulary, such as gable, sash or pediment, that they may have learnt.

It may be valuable to make a record of a building in a collaborative way. Where a building has regular repeating features it might be divided into vertical sections with one pupil responsible for each portion. Settle on a common scale and put the finished sections together to make a whole. Alternatively, working as a group pupils could each take responsibility for the careful recording of a feature such as doors, windows or chimneys and put them together later.

Using old pictures

Another way of focusing observation and recording of listed buildings is to provide pupils with an old picture of the building and its surroundings, and ask pupils to list any changes that have occurred and to think about what the changes would mean for the people living or working in or near the building. The reasons for the changes to the building can then be discussed.

Problem-solving roles

Using roles to help focus pupils on relevant information is a flexible method of conducting fieldwork. It is possible to create roles and problems identical to those faced in real life. Before the visit to a listed building set a problem. Suggest, for example, that a commercial company wants to turn the building into a leisure centre or the council wants to demolish it as part of a road-widening scheme or whatever else seems credible. Allocate roles such as developers, local planners, safety inspectors, or other roles taken from the Ryde Pavilion example, and ask pupils to look at the building through the eyes of that role with the idea of preparing a report or making a presentation.

Other types of role are possible. Pupils could be television producers planning a programme on the sad state of a local building. They could interview either the real-life people involved with the building or other pupils in their roles presenting a particular view. Pupils could be representatives of audio-tour companies planning taped guides for families, people with disabilities or foreign tourists. They could be novelists or playwrights or film makers collecting material for a setting for their work. It is up to you to determine the form of the final piece of work: it could be a tape, for example, or it could be written proposals, but the important point is that the purpose of the visit is clear and that pupils know the information and ideas they gather on the visit are to be used in some way afterwards. Remember also that because information was gathered whilst in a particular role this does not prevent it from being used in other contexts.

Buildings at risk

Many listed buildings are slowly decaying as a result of neglect. You might like to select a small local area that includes listed buildings to carry out a buildings at risk survey which could be computerised. The recording form opposite is currently in use by English Heritage and a booklet is available to explain some of the entries. Depending on the age of your pupils you will probably want to select part of the form and simplify it. Having decided on the scale of the problem of buildings at risk in your area, your pupils could contact the planning authority to see what work they have done in this field and then could discuss and campaign for appropriate ways of reviving the fortunes of specific buildings.

FURTHER RESEARCH

Listed buildings offer much potential for local history research since there is plentiful and varied documentary evidence about many of them in locally accessible archives. Research gives pupils the experience of handling, comprehending, and interpreting primary sources, evaluating, selecting, and editing relevant material. That the material is local and relevant will add to its appeal to pupils. But if pupils are going to do this research themselves, you must first check that it is feasible - that the records office can accommodate pupils and allows them to handle the material, and that the material does actually exist.

Further research may be an integral part of a project on the building. It may well be necessary when constructing arguments for and against different proposals. After fieldwork, it may be used to find differences between the past and the present, to test hypotheses, to explain odd features. Documentary evidence may be used as stimulus material or to test pupils' understanding of the building. It may be used as part of a concluding display on the project. The *Resources* section at the end of this book suggests the types of document that may be useful and the places in which to look for them.

SURVEY FORM FOR BUILDINGS AT RISK REGISTER

1. IDENTIFICATION

COUNTY ....DISTRICT............................... PARISH ....

NGR .... PRIME REF NO (Greenback No)..

LOCALITY .... (List Entry No)................./..................../................

St No .... St Name ....

Building name..

2. ARCHITECTURAL OR HISTORIC INTEREST

Grade   : I
          : II *
          : II   [ ]
Unlisted : UL

No of Conservation Areas
(If not in
Conservation Area = O)   [ ]

3. BUILDING USE AND TYPE

	Broad function (RCHM Code)	Detailed building type (Wordlist)
ORIGINAL	....	....
LAST/PRESENT	....	....
Upper Floors	..........................(Optional)	

4. CONDITION (Not Applicable : 0)   OCCUPANCY   RISK CATEGORY

CONDITION		OCCUPANCY		RISK CATEGORY
Very Bad	: 1	Vacant : 1	→	1
		Partially occupied : 2		2
		Occupied : 3		
Poor	: 2	Vacant : 1	→	3
		Partially occupied : 2		
		Occupied : 3		
Fair	: 3	Vacant : 1	→	4
		Partially occupied : 2		
		Occupied : 3		5
Good	: 4	Vacant : 1		
		Partially occupied : 2		6
		Occupied : 3		

CONDITION [ ]

OCCUPANCY [ ]

RISK CATEGORY [ ]

9. REPORTER'S NAME

5. OWNERSHIP TYPE

Private	: 1
Religious / Charity	: 2
Company	: 3
Local Authority	: 4
Statutory Undertaker	: 5
Crown	: 6

[ ]

**SECTION BELOW TO BE FILLED IN ONLY FOR
RISK CATEGORIES 1 - 3**
or Other Buildings of Concern

6. MARKET STATUS

For Sale   : Y
Not For Sale : N   [ ]

7. OWNERSHIP   Details of Owner / Agent

Name

Address

8. MARKET DETAILS

Asking Price   :
(As At Date)   :
Floor Area   :
Sq M   : M   :
Sq Ft   : F

10. REASON BUILDING AT RISK

11. PREFERRED USES

12. ACTION

LISTED BUILDINGS ACROSS THE CURRICULUM

CROSS-CURRICULAR SKILLS AND THEMES

The great strength of using listed buildings as a school topic is that it breaks down subject boundaries and teaches a wide range of skills and themes that are relevant to life. However, today's crowded school curriculum with its subjects competing for time dictates that any topic be justified by contribution to specific areas of the curriculum.

Listed buildings are ideal topics for three of the five National Curriculum cross-curricular themes: environmental education, citizenship (personal, community, national, including legal and political dimensions) and economic/ industrial understanding. Any of the activities suggested in the previous chapters would directly satisfy the statutory and non-statutory requirements in this area, whether as a primary topic, as a secondary Personal and Social Education course, or as part of a curriculum subject.

Listed buildings can be used as a starting point for spin-offs into almost any area of the curriculum or to pull together several seemingly disparate areas. The ideas set out below are only a fraction of the possibilities for integrated or follow-up work.

ENGLISH

Many starting points for creative or technical writing can be found amongst the suggestions for role play/problem-solving in fieldwork. For example, the material collected in the journalist role could be used in a variety of ways: as a newspaper article, a video docu-drama, a radio article or play, an exhibition/display, or as the basis for class discussion. Although most of the roles call for technical report writing, the collection of material for a story or drama production calls for the imaginative use of language. Additionally, poems (perhaps in appropriate shapes) can be written

Thorney Primary School, Cambridgeshire, have made their involvement with the local amenity society the focus of work in all areas of the curriculum. Pupils have been involved with the local museum, the village environment, historical festivals and the local council.

Thorney Primary School pupils meet the Mayor.

Polystyrene print of Thorney Abbey.

to illustrate or support arguments for alternative solutions for a building, and exercises on similes, metaphors, and even alliteration, can be used to spice up the arguments or campaigns.

e.g. The house is as rotten as..............
The house is as beautiful as...............
The house is as useless as ....
The house is beautiful, brilliant, ...and...........................
(think of two more beginning with a 'b')

MATHS

The surveying of buildings means practice in measuring, calculating heights, lengths, angles, areas and volumes. Pupils can be taught to calculate height by using a clinometer and length by measuring a short length (a person, ruler, book) and then multiplying. Where appropriate buildings can be surveyed using the historical measures - rods, perches and chains - instead of the modern metric system.

Buildings are excellent subjects for the study of shapes. Tessellation work can be done with floor tiles, brick patterns, window lattices, stained glass, and roofing tiles. The facades of buildings often illustrate a wide variety of shapes, lines and curves, and classical buildings provide excellent examples of symmetry. Scaffolding provides scope for structural geometry, and if the rooms and furniture of the interior can be accurately mapped, pupils can be asked to plan rearrangements of the furniture to fit different circumstances or functions.

The financial and statistical aspects of buildings provide opportunities for maths. Building costs, grants statistics and results of fieldwork surveys can be analysed, compared, and presented in graph or chart form.

SCIENCE

Many listed buildings can be used to help pupils understand force: barns are particularly useful because their internal structure can usually be clearly seen and churches' flying buttresses show graphically the problems of supporting heavy roofs. Old buildings may also have a variety of types of brick course. The strength of a structure can be tested by experiment in the classroom. Toy bricks can be used to test the different strengths of brick patterns by building walls with different structure and subjecting them to comparable forces. Arches can be constructed and tested in the same way. During fieldwork pupils can look at the different types and uses of materials, and, using magnifying glasses, can examine the different textures and structures of materials and compare their qualities.

The decay of listed buildings is a good topic for experiments that show scientific methodology. Fieldwork observation may produce hypotheses about how and why some materials decay differently to others, and experiments can test them: wood, stone, plastic, iron and others can be subjected to a variety of monitored controlled attacks by dripping water, being buried, being dropped, being exposed to the elements, being shaken violently as if by heavy traffic, as well as being protected in different ways. The differing results can be compared and discussed, and remedies to prevent decay planned.

TECHNOLOGY

Domestic houses are complex systems with many related parts. Pupils can usefully investigate how these parts operate. Where appropriate pupils could study methods of closing and securing doors and windows, storing materials, protecting the face of a building from the weather, heating the interior, or draining water and sewage. Of course, more complex specialist machinery can be studied in mills powered by steam, tide, water or wind, or in lighthouses and warehouses, where working gears, levers and pulleys are clear to see. Alternative improved systems can be designed, constructed and evaluated.

The Technology curriculum requires pupils to think about the design of information systems. They can plan public routes through listed buildings taking into consideration the conflicting needs to protect the building as well as give access to the public, and devise guidebooks or information panels to tell people about significant features. A trail round local listed buildings would also require careful design and planning.

An eroded statue on St Paul's Cathedral: the lead plugs on the coping were originally flush with the stone surface, which has eroded more quickly - 20mm in 270 years.

Scientists have concluded that stonework is surprisingly insensitive to the acidity of rainfall and that the rate at which it dissolves depends more on the volume of rainfall.

Stott Bobbin Mill. Machinery, especially if it is in working order, illustrates many technological principles.

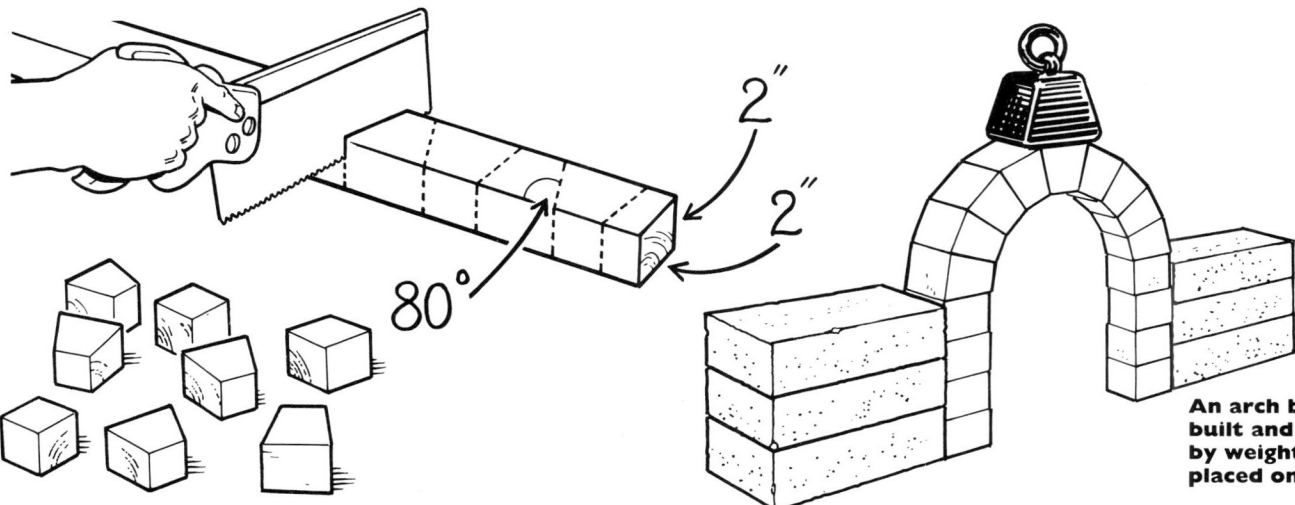

An arch being built and tested by weights placed on it.

The most obvious application for information technology and listed buildings is work with databases. The data used can be published material such as areas of the 1851 and other censuses which are available on disc. Many local record offices have records on listed buildings stored on disc. However, the pupils' fieldwork may well provide more suitable data for this work.

Using a Concept Keyboard the programme *Touch Explorer Plus* provides the opportunity to construct five levels of questions or information on every square of a grid overlaying a photograph of a building. Dataloggers are computer programmes linked to measuring apparatus and can be used to record and analyse anything that can be measured. This could be very useful when surveying the state of a listed building: inside, the damp, light and heat could be measured and logged, whilst outside the heat (to check insulation), air pollution and noise could be logged. The datalogging can provide material for database work.

ART

There are many different ways to portray the same building: photographs taken from different angles and distances with different lenses and filters, sketches varying from sentimental impressions to hard, stark, functional line drawings, tactile collages attempting to recreate the different surfaces of the building, rubbings of surfaces, and the different technical architectural projections. A class with experience of a variety of media can be set to produce a range of portrayals of the building.

GEOGRAPHY

The study of a local listed building can be the focus for a local study. Mapwork skills can be exercised by making or studying plans of the building, and old and current maps of its immediate environs. It may be appropriate to study the human geography of the area and how the building fits into local patterns of land-use and development as well as how the building materials reflect the local physical geography. Having identified what makes the locality distinct, pupils can discuss how far they are prepared to protect their environment to retain it.

HISTORY

Listed buildings are relevant to certain core study units and to some supplementary study units including the local history units. They can illuminate most of the British History units and they are currently suitable for GCSE coursework.

Buildings are tangible primary evidence of the past, and are useful to point up continuity and change. Younger pupils can compare an old building with their own house. Some listed buildings show clearly by their adaptation how fashions and lifestyles have changed.

Details from different eras noted by pupils can be charted on a timeline and displayed. An imagined interview

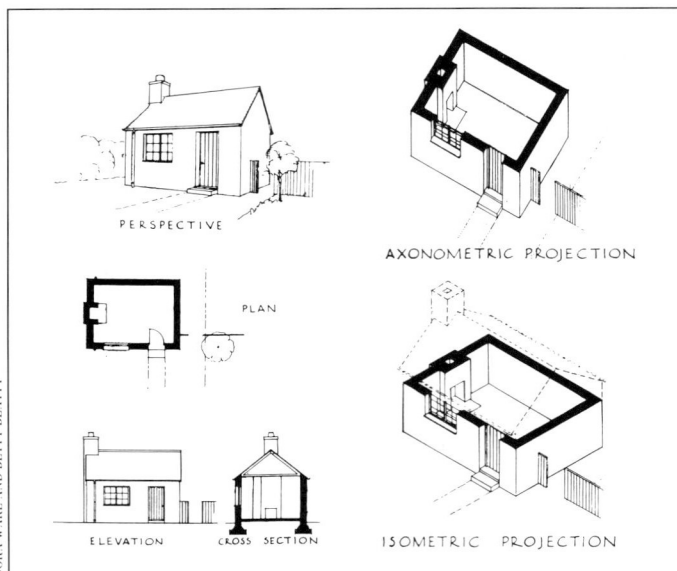

Listed buildings may often provide a good setting for

historical re-enactment. Here pupils are using Kirby Hall.

Pupils of Eckington School in Derbyshire have been involved in the regeneration of their local environment as part of their GCSE history coursework. This has involved detailed observation, and learning about the features of the buildings, using correct terminology.

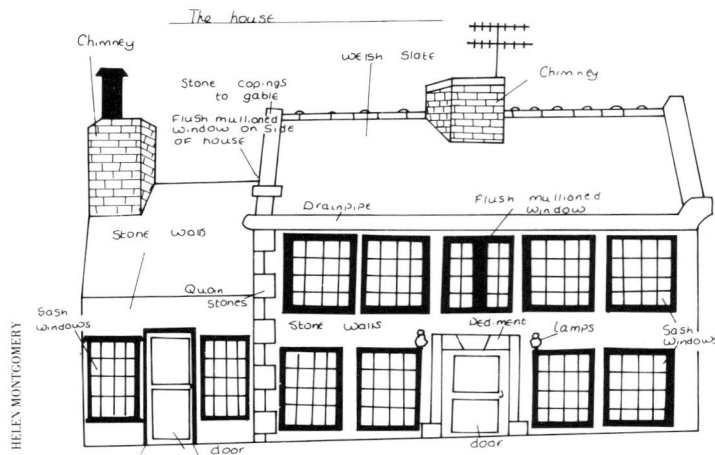

Different architectural projections of a listed building can be attempted by a team of older pupils, who can then analyse how each projection shows more, less, or different information about the building.

with the original owner, whether written or taped, can bring out continuity and change.

For older pupils the task will be more sophisticated. They can start to analyse choice of building materials, layout and style, and tease from this the attitudes and ideas of the time. Some questions that can be asked include: Which rooms inter-connect with each other? How open plan or private are the rooms? What do the windows overlook, or how overlooked by outside are they? What do the decorations or contents of the rooms tell us? What does the building tell us about the people who built it, lived in it or preserved it?

RESOURCES AND BIBLIOGRAPHY

There is a wide range of resources available if you want to research your local listed buildings and you will need to pick and choose according to the direction your work is taking and the age of your pupils.

GETTING STARTED

Local planning authority The offices of the local planning authority have already been mentioned as a good place to start research on listed buildings. As well as the possibility of there being an education or conservation officer who may be able to guide teachers or pupils with research, the offices will have the lists of protected buildings and large-scale maps.

Newspapers and television Since the most interesting stories about listed buildings are often the current ones, local and national newspapers are a fertile source for teachers. Television programmes can be useful: single documentaries and series on buildings and related issues are quite common, and relevant local news items can be quite frequent.

PLACES TO VISIT

County archaeology unit Your area may have a local archaeological unit which keeps records of all historical sites, covering not just the distant past but all sites up to and including the present century.

County Record Office For primary documentary sources, for maps, and possibly census returns, the County Record Office will be a key source. Contact the archivists well in advance of a visit since research facilities are often heavily booked.

Reference or local studies library Find out which of your local libraries maintains a local studies collection. This will have a wealth of secondary sources and may also keep a collection of old pictures.

Local museum Local museums may contain related artefacts. Since

TOPHAM PICTURE SOURCE

Appropriate photographs will help bring the study of a house to life. This house was built without a bathroom.

not all material will be on display it is worth asking curators if they have relevant material.

DOCUMENTARY SOURCES

The following section lists some of the main types of document that may contribute to your study.

Maps Maps can give pupils a useful visual history of how the contexts of listed buildings have changed. The Ordnance Survey began its work in the nineteenth century and facsimile versions of the first maps are sold today. The more recent 25 inches to the mile maps are a useful scale for studies of groups of buildings. Tithe maps, usually compiled in the 1840s, show all the houses in a parish, and are a rich source of names of landowners, houses, roads and even fields, all of which help to build up a picture of a building's past.

Census returns The first population census for England and Wales was taken in 1801 and after that at ten-year intervals. Up until

1831 the surviving documents are largely statistical and so of little use for research on specific listed buildings. The returns for the last hundred years are unavailable for inspection, but the returns for the years 1841-1891 will give the names, relationships, ages and occupations of all inhabitants at any given address.

Deeds, wills and inventories Deeds, wills and inventories will often give valuable information about the history of a house, but they may be in writing and language that are very difficult for pupils to decipher. Wills before about 1740 are often accompanied by inventories of the owner's household goods and equipment, even stating in which room each item is kept. Even if you cannot find an inventory for your building, it may be useful looking at others for an idea of the kind of interior that it might have had. If your building has recently been sold, it may be possible to obtain estate agent's particulars.

Trade directories Trade directories are early versions of the Yellow Pages: they contain all kinds of information about local and commercial life. If your building was a commercial one, you are likely to find it in a trade directory, together with its function and owner. Some areas were served by eighteenth-century directories, but White's directories (from 1845) and Kelly's directories (from the late nineteenth century) are the most useful series.

People's memories It is important with all local research to talk to as many people as possible, since so much local historical knowledge remains anecdotal. A letter to the local newspaper or a request for information broadcast on local radio can get numerous responses, and a class of pupils asking the old people of their street can unearth all sorts of interesting information that has not yet made it into print.

BIBLIOGRAPHY

The listing process
Anthony, B, 'Historic buildings: listing past and future', Manchester Literary and Philosophical Society in **Manchester conservation: the way forward**, 1987, ISBN 0-902428-09-8. Interesting and comprehensive story of listing.

Department of the Environment typescripts, March 1990: 1. 'What listing means - a guide for owners and occupiers'. 2. 'How to appeal against listing'. Available from local planning offices.

Department of the Environment, **Circular 8/87 Historic buildings and conservation areas: policy and procedures**, 1987, ISBN 0-11-751939-1. This covers directives and guidance on all issues associated with listing.

Ross, M, **Planning and the heritage: policy and problems**, E & F M Spon, 1990, ISBN 0-419-15100-1. Useful summary of history of legislation and an outline of procedures.

Suddards, R, **Listed buildings: the law and practice of historic buildings, ancient monuments and conservation areas**, Sweet and Maxwell, 1988 (2nd ed), ISBN 0-421-38130-2. Standard textbook.

The issues
Binney, M, **Our vanishing heritage**, Arlington, 1984, ISBN 0-85140-653-1. An account of campaigns to save a wide variety of types of building.

Catt, R, 'Listing a building often means important compromises', **Valuer** 58 (3), 1989. Puts forward the view that listing is a luxury of the rich, leaving no room for architectural innovation, and necessitating compromises on safety.

Fawcett, J (ed), **The future of the past: attitudes to conservation 1174-1974**, Thames and Hudson, 1976, ISBN 0-500-23231-8

Hewison, R, **The heritage industry: Britain in a climate of decline**, Methuen, 1987, ISBN 0-413-16110-2. An argument against the preservation that distorts and sanitizes our history for tourism.

Lowenthal, D, **The past is a foreign country**, Cambridge University Press, 1985, ISBN 0-521-22480-0. An excellent general work on the philosophy of history, and what, how and why we preserve.

Pearce, D, **Conservation today**, Routledge, 1989, ISBN 0-415-03914-2. A survey of recent building conservation in Britain.

Pyke, B, **The good looking house**, Redcliffe Press, 1980, ISBN 0-905459-23-7. Very useful on appropriate and inappropriate changes to groups of houses.

How to act
Binney, M and Watson-Smyth, M, **The SAVE Britain's heritage action guide**, Collins and Brown, 1991, ISBN 1-85585-056-7. How to campaign to save a building together with case studies.

The Georgian Group, **The Georgian Group advisory leaflets**: 1. Windows; 2. Georgian brickwork; 3. Georgian doors; 4. Paint colour; 5. Render, stucco and plaster; 6. Wallpaper; 7. Mouldings; 8. Ironwork. Available from the Georgian Group. See address list. Intended to guide house owners on maintenance and repair but containing much useful historical background.

Weir, H, **How to rescue a ruin: by setting up a local buildings preservation trust**, Architectural Heritage Fund, 1989, ISBN 0-9515468-0-5. Detailed advice.

Architectural history
Brunskill, R, **Illustrated handbook of vernacular architecture**, Faber and Faber, 1987, ISBN 0-571-13916-7. Good on details of buildings, useful photos, sketches, maps. Useful appendix with methodology for studying buildings.

Clifton-Taylor, A, **The pattern of English building**, Faber, 1972, ISBN 0-571-09525-9. A large, comprehensive volume on styles and materials of English architecture.

Girouard, M, **Life in the English country house: a social and architectural history**, Yale, 1978, ISBN 0-300-02273-5. Although concentrating on great historic houses, an excellent analysis of the relationship between the design and use of buildings.

Local architectural history
For almost any part of the country, there is a wealth of histories of local buildings, families and industries. In addition to books, journals of local historical and antiquarian societies often contain studies of local buildings.

The Victoria County History runs into several large volumes for most counties and covers the whole country.

Pevsner's **Buildings of England** also has volumes for every county and covers an enormous number of historical buildings.

The Survey of London, nearly a century in the compiling, is a comprehensive source for those areas covered by published volumes.

Ideas for teachers
Adams, E and Ward, C, **Art and the built environment**, Longman / Schools Council, 1982, ISBN 0-582-36195-8. Full of interesting ideas, especially for secondary school art, but applicable more widely.

Corbishley, M, 'The case of the blocked window', **Remnants, Journal of the English Heritage Education Service** 2, 1986. Suggests ways of looking at and recording changes to buildings.

Davis, J, 'Our house', **Primary Teaching Studies** 3, 1987. Primary pupils' investigative project, involving topics across many areas of the curriculum.

Durbin, G, 'Using photographs: exteriors', **Remnants, Journal of the English Heritage Education Service** 8, Summer 1989, and 'Using photographs: interiors', **Remnants** 7, Spring 1989. Ideas on how to use photographs of buildings with pupils.

Durbin, G, Morris, S and Wilkinson, S, **A teacher's guide to learning from objects**, English Heritage, 1990, ISBN 1-85074-259-6. Suggests a method of analysing objects and a range of classroom games to help develop the skills that are necessary for fieldwork at sites or museums.

Iredale, D, **Discovering your old house**, Shire, 1977, ISBN 0-85263-402-1. Good small book with ideas on how to research old buildings.

Norman, B, **Portsea workhouse**, Archaeology and Education Project, Department of Archaeology, University of Southampton, 1988, ISBN 0-85432-295-7.

Steane, J, **Upstanding archaeology**, Council for British Archaeology, ISSN 0262-897-X. Detailed advice on what to look for in a whole range of types of building, interior and exterior.

Books for pupils

Ellis, R and C, **Windows**, Bodley Head, 1975, ISBN 0-370-01587-8. Ideas for a primary topic focusing on windows.

Gee, A, **Looking at houses**, Batsford, 1983, ISBN 0-7134-0845-6. A very useful look at individual features, with good diagrams. For secondary pupils.

Marshall, P, **Houses and homes**, MacDonald, 1985, ISBN 0-356-10145-2. An excellent set of archive photographs 1850-1960, with a short commentary, on houses and their occupants. Useful for all ages.

Neal, P, **The urban scene**, Dryad, 1987, ISBN 0-8521-9685-7. Good on all aspects of pressures and changes to the urban character and environment. For key stages 2, 3 and 4.

Swift, K, **Homes**, Longman, 1991, ISBN 0-582-04018-3. Introduction to historical sources for key stage 1.

Whitlock, R, **Exploring buildings**, Wayland, 1987, ISBN 1-85210-002-8. Ideas for a local project for pupils in key stages 2 and 3.

Audio-visual resources

Handing on our history, English Heritage, 1990, 30 mins. Introduction to the work of English Heritage, suitable for 6th forms. Available from English Heritage Postal Sales.

Protectors of our past, English Heritage, 1989, 16 mins. A non-technical video summary of conservation of buildings, the diversity of problems, and strategies for solving them. Available from English Heritage Postal Sales.

The archaeological detectives, English Heritage, 1990, 20 mins. Suggests a method for observing buildings and making deductions from observation. Two primary pupils investigate a Roman city, a castle and an eighteenth-century house. Available from English Heritage Postal Sales.

Clues challenge, English Heritage, 1990, 14 mins. Two children visit modern locations familiar to them and apply detective skills which can be developed later on visits to historic buildings. Available from English Heritage Postal Sales.

Houses and homes, Acorn Media.

The Development of the Domestic House, Slide Centre. Both these slide sets are available from the Slide Centre. Contact:
The Slide Centre
Ilton
Ilminster
Somerset TA19 9HS

Maps

Ordnance Survey county maps from 1850 and various London and Home County maps of 1800-1910 available from:
Stanfords Ltd
12-14 Long Acre
London WC2E 9LP
Tel: 071-836 1321

CONTACTS

English Heritage Education Service. The regional officers may be able to help schools with projects. The section produces a variety of teachers' books and videos and also runs courses for teachers. Free publications available are **Remnants**, a journal for schools published termly, **Information for teachers**, and **Resources**, a catalogue of educational materials. It can also supply copies of the English Heritage **Conservation Bulletin**. Contact:
English Heritage Education Service
Keysign House
429 Oxford Street
London W1R 2HD
Tel: 071-973 3442/3

Royal Commission on the Historical Monuments of England. This organisation's main task is to survey England's architectural and archaeological heritage. Its Threatened Buildings Section records all types of historic buildings threatened with demolition or alteration. All the information is kept in their public archive, the National Buildings Record, which has an extensive photograph library arranged by parish. It also has a complete set of all the listed building lists. Contact:
Royal Commission on the Historical Monuments of England
Fortress House
23 Savile Row
London WIX 2JQ
Tel: 071-973 3064

ROYAL COMMISSION ON THE HISTORICAL MONUMENTS OF ENGLAND

The Lloyd's Building, London. A candidate for future listing?

Department of the Environment, Listing Branch. Publishes factual details about listing, and deals with applications for spot listing. Contact:
Listing Branch
Department of the Environment
2 Marsham Street
London SW1P 3EB
Tel: 071-276 6456

Civic Trust. The umbrella organisation for 950 local amenity societies from all round the country, campaigning over local building and environmental issues. It has links with local planning offices, and runs its own schools magazine, **Shaping**

Place, and adult magazine, **Heritage Outlook**. Contact:
Education Officer
Civic Trust
17 Carlton House Terrace
London SW1Y 5AW
Tel: 071-930 0914

Georgian Group. Campaigns to save Georgian buildings, advises on the restoration of them, and promotes appreciation of Georgian and classical heritage. Produces a list of publications which includes a series of reports on Georgian towns under threat from unsympathetic development and some useful advisory leaflets on details of Georgian architecture.
Contact:
Georgian Group
37 Spital Square
London E1 6DY
Tel: 071-377 1722

Royal Institute of British Architects. Runs an **Architects-in-schools** scheme. Contact:
Royal Institute of British Architects
66 Portland Place
London W1N 4AD
Tel: 071-580 5533

Royal Town Planning Institute. Has an Environmental Education Panel which promotes links between planners and schools. Contact:
Environmental Education Panel
Royal Town Planning Institute
26 Portland Place
London W1N 4BE
Tel: 071-636 9107

SAVE Britain's Heritage. Campaigns to save endangered historic buildings, and has an excellent selection of publications - 88 in the current catalogue. Contact:
SAVE Britain's Heritage
68 Battersea High Street
London SW11 3HX
Tel: 071-228 3336

Society for the Protection of Ancient Buildings. The oldest and one of the largest organisations with a wide range of activities and publications including information and technical advice sheets. Contact:
Society for the Protection of Ancient Buildings
37 Spital Square
London E1 6DY
Tel: 071-377 1644

Thirties Society. Promotes the conservation of inter-war architecture. Contact:
Thirties Society
58 Crescent Lane
London SW4 9PU
Tel: 071-738 8480

Victorian Society. Campaigns and publishes to save Victorian and Edwardian buildings, and to promote their appreciation. Contact:
Victorian Society
1 Priory Gardens
London W4 1TT
Tel: 081-994 1019

ACKNOWLEDGEMENTS

We are grateful to the following people for help in producing this book: Kim Carr, Celia Clark, Rosemary Cooper, Margaret Fletcher and Bob Hawkins.

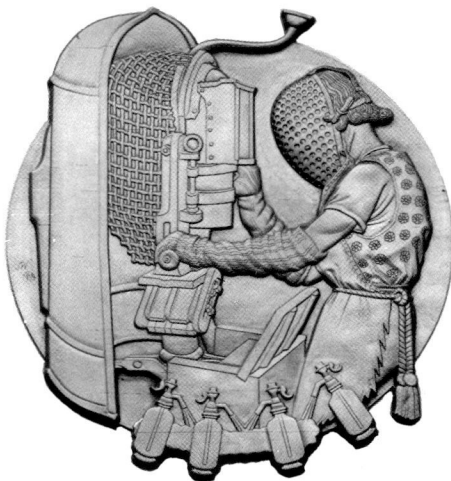

Detail from the door of Norwich City Hall, a Grade II listed building, celebrating the local soft drinks manufacture.

ROYAL COMMISSION ON THE HISTORICAL MONUMENTS OF ENGLAND